The Unified Ring
Narrative Art and the
Science-Fiction Novel

Studies in Speculative Fiction, No. 11

Robert Scholes, Series Editor

Alumni/Alumnae Professor of English and
Chairman, Department of English
Brown University

Other Titles in This Series

No. 1	*Feminist Futures: Contemporary Women's Speculative Fiction*	Natalie M. Rosinsky
No. 2	*Ray Bradbury and the Poetics of Reverie: Fantasy, Science Fiction, and the Reader*	William F. Touponce
No. 3	*The Scientific World View in Dystopia*	Alexandra Aldridge
No. 4	*Approaches to the Fiction of Ursula K. Le Guin*	James W. Bittner
No. 5	*Utopia: The Psychology of a Cultural Fantasy*	David Bleich
No. 6	*Biological Themes in Modern Science Fiction*	Helen N. Parker
No. 8	*Scientific Attitudes in Mary Shelley's* Frankenstein	Samuel Holmes Vasbinder
No. 9	*The Novels of Philip K. Dick*	Kim Stanley Robinson
No. 10	*The Politics of Fantasy: C.S. Lewis and J.R.R. Tolkien*	Lee D. Rossi
No. 12	*Science, Myth, and the Fictional Creation of Alien Worlds*	Albert Wendland

The Unified Ring
Narrative Art and the Science-Fiction Novel

by
Frank Sadler

UMI RESEARCH PRESS
Ann Arbor, Michigan

Copyright © 1984, 1974
Frank Orin Sadler
All rights reserved

Produced and distributed by
UMI Research Press
an imprint of
University Microfilms International
A Xerox Information Resources Company
Ann Arbor, Michigan 48106

Library of Congress Cataloging in Publication Data

Sadler, Frank.
 The unified ring.

 (Studies in speculative fiction ; no. 11)
 Revision of thesis (Ph.D.)–University of Florida,
1974.
  Bibliography: p.
  Includes index.
  1. Science fiction–Technique. 2. Narration (Rhetoric)
I. Title. II. Series.
PN3377.5.S3S2 1984   809.3'876   84-16232
ISBN 0-8357-1598-1 (alk.paper)

To both my children
John Samuel and Brook Jenkins Sadler
and my former wife
Catherine Anne Selleg

Contents

Preface *ix*

Acknowledgments *xi*

Introduction *xiii*

1 Narrative Technique and the World View *1*

2 Relativity and the Universe of Fiction *19*

3 Probability and the Principle of Uncertainty *45*

4 Time and the Structure of Reality *73*

5 A Wholistic Theory of the Science-Fiction Novel *91*

Notes *105*

Bibliography *111*

Index *115*

Preface

In the ten years since the preponderance of this book was first written, little has taken place to warrant optimism about the future of science-fiction criticism. What has been published, for the most part, continues to be rather traditional in its examination of the science-fiction novel.

Developments in semiotics and deconstructionist theory have largely gone unnoticed and unexamined. The valuable work of a scholar such as Robert Scholes has yet to find its way into the criticism of science fiction. I had hoped for a renaissance in science-fiction criticism. Yet none seems to have emerged and, for a variety of reasons, I am doubtful about the future. Science fiction continues to be the step-child of the novel and mainstream criticism. Nevertheless, I believe that the scholarly study of science fiction can teach us much about the novel and criticism.

Art, whether it is visual or literary, continues to provide us with our raison d'être. It shapes and controls our fictions in ways which are non-reductive and leaves the essential mysteries of life untouched. My method is somewhat eclectic and personal. I offer no apologies for it. It is, in one sense, intellectual, while in another, truly creative.

Acknowledgments

This book is dedicated to all those teachers who helped to shape the growth of my imagination and thought and who continue to influence my life. I am especially in debt to the following individuals:

William R. Robinson, whose philosophy of life and literature continues to call into question all that may be termed "traditional" in the study of criticism and art.

Charles Lewis Tatham, who kindly tolerated my wild and untempered enthusiasm for literature as an undergraduate student and who influenced me to pursue its study.

John William Ruff (deceased), who directed my early graduate studies of English and always allowed me enough "rope" to hang myself with.

Motley Deakin, who taught me the value of patience and careful attention to detail.

To these and many others I owe a great debt. Thank you.

Introduction

The subject of this book is science fiction and the effects of modern science on the form and structure of the science-fiction novel. I am concerned primarily with the narrative art of the science-fiction novel and not with its ideas per se. Yet the nature of science fiction demands that its ideas be explored fully, for it is a central premise of my book that the ideas and principles of modern science and especially those of modern mathematical physics have brought about profound changes in the way in which man sees himself in his universe and in his literature.

In recent years science fiction has become a form of popular literature read by an increasingly wide and diverse audience. However, the critical examination of science fiction as a legitimate and serious literature warranting scholarly attention has been late in coming. Only within the past ten or twenty years has any serious attention, other than an occasional essay, been devoted to the subject. Thomas D. Clareson in his "Introduction: The Critical Reception of Science Fiction" points out that "within the past decade or so science fiction has gained a narrow critical and academic respectability because of its concerns with utopian-dystopian themes."[1] There are, of course, a great many reasons why science fiction has not received a wider critical and academic respectability. As Clareson suggests, one reason is that

> "modern" science fiction has never completely overcome its popular origins in dime pulps featuring such titles as *Thrilling Wonder Stories, Astounding, Startling,* or *Super-Science Stories.* Because it [science fiction] has been confined to such magazines and their successors, there has grown up that short-sighted perspective which speaks of the genre only in terms of what has been published originally in these pulps.[2]

Perhaps a more important reason for the lack of critical attention paid to science fiction is that the writing of most science fiction has been dismally incompetent. Nevertheless, anyone who is seriously interested in the academic study of science fiction should read one of the recent histories of the genre by such authors as Sam Moskowitz (*Explorers of the Infinite* or *Seekers of Tomorrow*), Brian W. Aldiss (*Billion Year Spree*), or W. H. G. Armytage (*Yesterday's Tomorrows*), or turn to one of the recent critical volumes of essays which present a sample of scholarly activity such as Clareson's book mentioned above or Reginald Bretnor's *Science Fiction: Today and Tomorrow*. Also of great importance is *Extrapolation,* The Journal of the MLA Seminar on Science Fiction; *Riverside Quarterly,* published by Leland Sapiro; and a new scholarly *Science-Fiction Studies,* published by the Department of English, Indiana State University. The future promises a continued acceleration in the critical examination of science fiction. Yet it should be pointed out that science fiction, because of its particular nature, raises serious questions about traditional critical theories of literature. These questions raise doubts about the established methods of critical inquiry used in the examination of the novel and literature, and about such basic ideas as the nature of reality. In brief, it may be argued that science fiction calls into doubt all those areas of traditional critical concern in which tentative solutions have been found to specific problems. Science fiction questions what is meant by "science" and "fiction" and mirrors, to some degree, the two-culture phenomenon—the clash between science and the humanities or arts. Yet there exists a growing body of science fiction which exhibits an integrative tendency between these two areas, suggesting that, perhaps, a new literature is in the process of emerging, a literature as radically different, in certain ways, from nineteenth-century literature as Romantic literature was from the literature of the eighteenth century.

The intent of this book is to study the craft of recent science fiction. Because I believe that science fiction must *account* for its science, I have attempted to explore the various ramifications of modern mathematical physics as they are exemplified in the structure of the science-fiction novel. This has not been an easy task for one who has received his training primarily within the confines of English literature, for it has demanded that I learn something about the nature of the revolution that has occurred within the sciences in this century. I make no claim to be expert in the areas of modern mathematical physics I have had to explore, and I have found myself relying on the authoritative comments of others who are recognized as experts in their particular areas. However, this should not prohibit me from making certain observations about the nature of the principles involved and their applicability to the study of the science-fiction novel. For there can be no doubt that an understanding of science and scientific principles is necessary in order to fully understand the novels examined here. Without some understanding of the principles discussed in these novels, I doubt seriously whether they can be properly evaluated.

Each chapter in my study represents an examination of a set of principles taken from modern mathematical physics as they evidence themselves in the novels I have chosen to study. These principles illustrate various aspects of a way of looking at man and his universe which differs fundamentally from that of the last century. Consequently, in chapter 1 the relationship between narrative technique and the world view is examined. In chapter 2 my focus is on the theory of relativity and fiction; in chapter 3 I look at the Principle of Uncertainty and probability theory as they affect the structure of the novel; chapter 4 examines the nature of time and reality; and, finally, in chapter 5 I propose a wholistic theory of the science-fiction novel. Each of the novels selected as examples was chosen because it represents what I consider to be the best in the field with respect to narrative art and the ideas and concepts involved in its presentation. Though I concentrate on one particular aspect of each novel, that novel could also be examined at some length in terms of all the scientific principles I have discussed in this book.

1
Narrative Technique and the World View

The problems of modern art, so frequently and passionately discussed in our time, force us to examine those foundations which form the presuppositions for every development of art, foundations which at other times are taken as self-evident.

Werner Heisenberg

It is clear that each scientific reinterpretation of the physical universe has produced a corresponding reinterpretation in the literary arts. For instance, Marjorie Hope Nicholson's *The Breaking of the Circle* convincingly demonstrates the effects of the "new science" of Copernicus, Galileo, Newton, and Kepler on the artistic and philosophical ideas of the seventeenth century.[1] Arnold Hauser's "The Conceptions of Time in Modern Art and Science" traces the differing conceptions of time in relation to man's world view and shows how these various conceptions of time "reflect perhaps most conspicuously the points of contact between art and science, and allow us to describe the present situation in the closest connection with the past."[2] Likewise, Lois and Stephen Rose's *The Shattered Ring* analyzes the impact of modern science on man's quest for meaning through a study of contemporary science fiction.[3] Other studies, such as Alfred North Whitehead's *Science and the Modern World,* outline the effects of modern science on the philosophical thinking of our own day.[4] That modern science has produced a change in the way in which man understands and orients himself in the universe, no one would seriously question. Yet it is equally clear that little if any attention has been given to the various ways in which narrative technique has been influenced by modern science. The aim of this first chapter, then, is to study the indirect relation that exists between narrative technique and the world view of modern mathematical physics and to suggest that this relation may serve as the basis for creating a means by which changes in the art of the science-fiction novel may be evaluated.

There is no evidence or reason to believe that narrative technique has influenced our world view either directly or indirectly whereas there are a great many reasons for believing that the effects of modern science on literary art have been pervasive. Studies such as Wayne C. Booth's *The Rhetoric of Fiction* examine the possibilities and limitations of narrative technique in light of individual examples drawn from the universe of fiction.[5] Booth's study, though comprehensive, makes no attempt to understand the fictional devices of the novel with respect to how these devices have been shaped and influenced in their use in the novel by modern science. Booth simply presents a discussion of fictional devices as they have been used in the novel without, for the most part, attempting to show how these devices have changed as a result of shifts in our world view. Further, Booth is concerned primarily with discussing how various authors have handled narrative devices in the novel. In his chapter dealing with the "Types of Narration," Booth declares:

> Narration is an art, not a science, but this does not mean that we are necessarily doomed to fail when we attempt to formulate principles about it. There are systematic elements in every art, and criticism of fiction can never avoid the responsibility of trying to explain technical successes and failures by reference to general principles. But we must always ask where the general principles are to be found. (p. 164)

Booth's "principles," however, are not principles so much as they are observations of the various ways in which narrative devices have been used in the novel. They certainly are not principles in the same sense as principles exist in the sciences. Booth observes the usage of different fictional devices in the novel, discusses their usage, and attempts to classify them by the kinds of variations which exist between them. Booth's study is valuable because it establishes, in a sense, the raw data of observation upon which a set of principles may then be created while, at the same time, it attempts to establish a critical vocabulary for formulating principles. And Booth admits that his "principles" are only observations and that their definition is limited because of the complexity of the number of ways in which they have been used. He proceeds from a neutral position; that is, Booth simply observes what has taken place rather than arguing from a specific "philosophic" position in his discussion and examination of the ways in which fictional devices have been used.

Jean Paul Sartre, on the other hand, in "François Mauriac and Freedom," approaches the problem of the use of fictional devices in the narrative from an entirely different point of view.⁶ Sartre, in writing of Mauriac, argues that:

> Like most of our writers, he [Mauriac] has tried to ignore the fact that the theory of relativity applies in full to the universe of fiction, that there is no more place for a privileged observer in a real novel than in the world of Einstein, and that it is no more possible to conduct an experiment in a fictional system in order to determine whether the system is in motion or at rest than there is in a physical system. (p. 23)

In a very basic sense this passage from Sartre is a major source for the idea of this study and, therefore, is worth exploring in some depth. The assumption Sartre makes—and it is an important assumption—is that a fundamental change has occurred in the way in which man understands and perceives the physical universe and that this change has altered the way in which we must understand the use and function of various narrative devices (techniques) in any "fictional system." Further, Sartre assumes that it is possible validly to compare literary creations to the principles which govern reality; that is, we may compare imaginative creations to the way in which science perceives the physical universe. A less obvious result of this assumption, and a more important one, is that narrative technique must be appropriate to the world view, both implicit and explicit, as it exists in the novel. In commenting on Mauriac's fiction, Sartre is suggesting, albeit indirectly, that omniscient narration is inappropriate to the modern novel since the modern novel must take into account the theory of relativity if it is to be considered modern. In other words, Sartre is suggesting that the world view created by modern science establishes the parameters or limits of the possibilities within which fiction may function. From Sartre's point of view, Mauriac's art is out-of-date and not in keeping with more modern or recent theories of the novel. The use of a privileged observer, in Sartre's theory of the novel, is inappropriate to the way in which he sees the world and practices his art in it. Sartre, however, would probably not reject the idea of the limited use of a privileged observer under certain circumstances, since to do so would be to misunderstand the theory of relativity; that is, the theory of relativity does not reject or discard the older notion of a continuous and mechanistic universe, but simply states that it is a somewhat limited and special case within the theory of relativity. Put another way, what I am suggesting is that omniscient narration is appropriate to classical philosophy whereas, for instance, first person narration is better suited to the world of Einstein.

The point to be made here, though, is that neither Booth nor Sartre treat the central problem I have outlined at the beginning of this chapter, though Sartre's point of view provides us with a valuable and convenient way of introducing my subject. Where Booth approaches the study of fictional devices from what seems to be a neutral position, Sartre assumes, for various reasons, that the world view created by modern science does determine the appropriateness or inappropriateness of certain narrative devices, such as point of view and narrative time sequence, and their use in fiction. Booth observes and Sartre theorizes. The difference between these two critics lies in their starting points and, consequently, results in a different type of information about the nature of literary art.

Werner Heisenberg in "The Representation of Nature in Contemporary Physics" suggests that:

> Indeed, the question has been raised whether the relation of modern man toward nature differs so fundamentally from that of former times that this difference alone is responsible for a completely different point of departure for the fine arts in contemporary culture.[7]

The question Heisenberg raises in this passage is central to several assumptions made in this chapter, assumptions which are, perhaps, self-evident but, nevertheless, need to be stated. Obviously Sartre believes with Heisenberg that "the relation of modern man toward nature differs . . . fundamentally from that of former times" and "that this difference . . . is responsible for a completely different point of departure for the fine arts in contemporary culture." But to understand the various ways in which the contemporary world view of modern mathematical physics has shaped and influenced narrative technique in the science-fiction novel we must first restate the above opinion or belief as a conclusion: the relation of modern man toward nature has fundamentally altered and this alteration or change has resulted in a different way in which modern man sees himself and his place in the universe. After all, the advent of the nuclear age and of men on the moon not once but several times must indicate, even to the most unsophisticated observer, the revolutionary changes modern science has wrought in man's understanding of the physical world. As J. Bronowski points out in *The Common Sense of Science,* "Science today is plainly more powerful than, let us say, in the time of Isaac Newton."[8] The power of science, however, does not lie in its translation into technology but rather in "fact and thought giving strength to one another" (Bronowski, p. 99). In other words, modern science has effected a fundamental revolution, conceptually and ideationally, in the way it sees the universe. This revolution is responsible for a change in the way in which man sees and orients himself in the universe. After all, the fact of the matter is that the theories of modern science have resulted in momentous changes. Yet whether or not these changes in the way in which modern science sees the universe are, as Heisenberg questions, solely "responsible for a completely different point of departure for the fine arts in contemporary culture" will depend, in the final analysis, on whether or not we perceive them. Heisenberg's answer to this problem of seeing is qualified:

> We may believe that changes in the foundations of modern science are indicative of profound transformations in the fundamentals of our existence, which on their part certainly have their effects in all areas of human experience. From this point of view it may be valuable for the artist to consider what changes have occurred during the last decade in the scientific view of nature. (pp. 122–23)

Since the appearance of Jules Verne in the last century, this consideration of the changes that have taken place in science's view of nature has been the preoccupation of the writer of science fiction; it has been, perhaps, the major source for his ideas and beliefs about the nature of the world. However, this examination by writers such as Wells, Gernsback, Campbell, Clarke, Heinlein, and Isaac Asimov, has taken place primarily on the level of theme and idea in the novel and for the most part has not been reflected (until recently) in the art and craft of the science-fiction novel, that is, in its use of various narrative techniques. The reasons for this lie in part in the history of the development and evolution of science fiction as a distinct sub-genre of the novel and with the major concerns of the writers themselves. Gary K. Wolfe in "The Limits of Science Fiction" points out that it has been claimed that science fiction is the "only true literature of ideas, or the only 'relevant' literature . . . apart from non-fiction that is of any use at all."[9] Obviously, this is an extreme position and one which Wolfe himself claims is:

> common among 'defenders of the faith,' as it were, and . . . [is] perhaps a necessary feature of any literature that has long been ignored or even oppressed by the literary establishment. Once such a literature begins to win acceptance, however, such attitudes begin to sound rather shrill and hysterical. (p. 30)

In addition, a major reason for the apparent lack of concern for the art of science fiction is due to the fact that a great many of the writers of science fiction have had no training in literary art. They have received their experience in the grist mill of pulp-publication which has not been tolerant of experimentation. However, a more fundamental and serious reason for the relative lack of sophistication in the narrative art of the science-fiction novel lies at the very point where such writers as Isaac

Asimov make their claim for science fiction as the literature of ideas. What I mean to imply is that these writers have not become fully aware (for various reasons) of what is inherent in the very ideas they claim to treat in their fiction. That is, they apparently conceive of the novel as simply a vehicle for working out the implications of certain ideas taken from the sciences and for studying their hypothetical applications to man and his society without realizing that the vehicle itself may be an inadequate one for expressing these ideas.

Obviously some writers are more aware than others of the changes that have taken place in man's understanding of the physical universe. Judith Merril in her essay "What Do You Mean: Science? Fiction?" declares:

> "Man is the *proper* study of any artist—man and" . . . etc. Call it the Bretnor-Merril Uncertainty Principle: you cannot define or describe a man except in terms of the universe of which he is aware; you cannot define or describe the universe except in terms of man's orientation within it.[10]

Merril's statement is conditioned, in part, by the idea of awareness—man's awareness of the universe and his place or orientation in it. Properly speaking, Merril is enunciating a point of view and a set of ideas which express a philosophy of understanding about the nature of man and the universe which is held currently by contemporary physics. She is doing so, however, from the point of view of that philosophy's relevance to the artist in his study of man. It would appear, then, that Sartre, for instance, is more aware of the changes which have taken place and of their implications for literary art than is, let us say, Mauriac. Science fiction, then, because it purports to explore the effects of modern science on man's existence, should reveal the degree and depth to which these effects have wrought changes in the art of the science-fiction novel. Further, as Merril points out:

> The literature of the mid-20th century can be meaningful only in so far as it perceives, and relates itself to, the central reality of our culture: the revolution in scientific thought which has replaced mechanics with dynamics, classification with relativity, certainties with statistical probabilities, dualism with parity. (p. 54)

Because science fiction purports to deal with the "central reality of our culture" by describing, as H. Bruce Franklin suggests in *Future Perfect*, the "present reality in terms of a credible hypothetical invention—past, present, or, most usually future—extrapolated from that reality," it would seem to become the logical place to find experiments, for instance, with the narrative time sequence of the novel and its relation to the various types of fictional devices and their function in the science-fiction novel.[11] But in fact most science fiction and most criticism of science fiction has been concerned primarily with an exploration of its ideational content and has paid little or no attention to science fiction as an art. In chapter 4 I will discuss Kurt Vonnegut Jr.'s *Slaughterhouse-Five* as one of the major exceptions to the absence of experimentation with the narrative time sequence of the novel. Further, as Wolfe suggests in his essay:

> In the term "science fiction," "fiction" itself becomes a merely decorative framework for rational speculation, controlled by the key term "science." Carried to its logical extent, such an attitude produces works such as Gernsback's *Ralph 124C 41+*, impressive in terms of scientific extrapolation, but dismally incompetent in terms of even the most elementary fictional techniques—and practically unread today. (p. 32)

Unfortunately, Wolfe is correct, which complicates the problem. In brief, it may be stated that the history of the development of the science-fiction novel has paralleled the development of the novel. However, this development in some ways has been compressed in time to less than one hundred years.[12] In other words, the development of the science-fiction novel has simply recapitulated the development of the novel, stopping that development somewhere toward the end of the nineteenth century. It is only in the last two decades (roughly) that the science-fiction novel has begun to emerge as a truly experimental form for such writers as Samuel R. Delany, Brian Aldiss, and Kurt Vonnegut, Jr. One work from each of these writers is treated in chapters 2, 3, and 4, respectively.

In discussing the problem of the relation of the world view to that of narrative technique, it is essential that we understand one of the major philosophical points that arises from Einstein's work. Jacob Bronowski points out that "Relativity derives essentially from the philosophic analysis which insists that there is not a fact and an observer, but a joining of the two in an observation. This is the fundamental unit of physics: the actual observation" (p. 78). The consequence of this philosophic analysis is what seems to be at the heart of Sartre's position on Mauriac and forms the necessary foundation or presupposition for recent developments in the art of the science-fiction novel. Presumably, the fiction of the eighteenth and nineteenth centuries was marked in its broad outline by various forms of omniscient narration, of which Mauriac's "privileged observer" is a variant, the use of first person narration and, as Alain Robbe-Grillet suggests in *For A New Novel,* the "systematic use of the past tense and the third person, unconditional adoption of chronological development, linear plots, regular trajectory of the passions, impulse of each episode toward a conclusion."¹³ According to Robbe-Grillet, in this earlier fiction, "Everything tended to impose the image of a stable, coherent, continuous, unequivocal, entirely decipherable universe" (p. 30). This characterization of narrative technique is in a sense the logical outcome of a mechanistic theory of the universe, of a world view which is, at its heart, Newtonian. Underlying this outline of the characteristics of the nineteenth-century novel is an objective concept of time. Arnold Hauser in his essay (mentioned briefly at the beginning of this chapter) points out that:

> In the age of classical cosmology, that is, in the sixteenth and seventeenth centuries, the prevailing conception of time is essentially mathematical and mechanistic. Time is an objective, independent and indifferent, continuous and homogeneous medium, a kind of reservoir which receives and holds all occurrences without influencing them and without being influenced, colored, quickened, or slowed down by them. Time is in the mechanistic theories of the universe an index, a mere accident of matter; material reality remains essentially unchanged by the passing of time—it merely locates an event in relation to other events; and time as a whole is but the configuration of instantaneous occurrences or the sum total of single moments; in a word, a line formed by the juxtaposition of points. (p. 322)

As Hauser points out, time was conceived of as a linear progression from moment to moment. Ronald W. Clark notes in *Einstein: The Life and Times* that:

> In the first pages of his [Newton's] *Philosophiae Naturalis Principia Mathematica,* . . . Newton used two words whose definition formed the basis not only of his whole system but of everything which had been constructed as a by-product of it—two words which between them formed the bottom layer of the house which science had been building for two and a half centuries. One of them was "time," the other was "space." "Absolute, true, and mathematical time," as Newton put it, "of itself and from its own nature, flows equably, without relation to anything external, and by another name is called duration."¹⁴

Further, according to Clark, "Space could be 'absolute space, in its own nature, without relation to anything external,' which 'remains always similar and immovable': or relative space, which [is] 'some movable dimension or measure of the absolute spaces' " (p. 75). Newton's formulation of the absolute nature of time and space resulted in the "searching conception of the universe as a machine: not a pattern but a clockwork" (Bronowski, p. 31). Newton's conception of time and space became the dominant idea which formed the base of the world view of the eighteenth and nineteenth centuries. This Newtonian conception of time became, in the novel, the major structuring device that gave order to the "events" which were reported there. This is what Robbe-Grillet means when he speaks of the "systematic use of past tense and the third person, unconditional adoption of chronological development, linear plots," etc. Unlike Einstein, Newton's analysis insisted on a philosophic separation between "a fact and an observer." This explains to some degree the absence of experiments, for instance, in the narrative time sequence of the science-fiction novel and it does so since, for the most part, the writers of science fiction have simply adopted the form of the nineteenth-century novel. It is no accident, then, that the novel which began "I was born . . ." as Robbe-Grillet tells us, reached the apogee of its development in the nineteenth century (p. 130). Further, it should be pointed out that since the predominant world view was mechanistic (not organic) and Newton had believed that "space represented the divine omnipresence of God in nature," then omniscient narration should be prominent during this period (Barnett, p. 40). For this world view permitted, analogically as a logical consequence of its postulation, omniscient narration in fiction. In addition to this Robbe-Grillet comments that the "composition of the novel of the nineteenth-century type which was life itself a hundred years ago, is no longer anything but an empty formula, serving only as the basis for tiresome parodies" (p. 135). Whether or not the *formula* is empty is of little consequence. What is important is the formula itself, for the formula was the product of a world view which came into being during the seventeenth century and had its climax at the end of the nineteenth. What happened in science fiction with the advent of a new world view, as created by modern science, was almost without exception a continuation of the form of the novel of the nineteenth-century type while the writer used this form as a vehicle to discuss the new ideas of science and their significance for man. The science-fiction novel of the first half of the twentieth century shows little or no modification or development from its ancestry. The form of the novel remained essentially unchanged while the ideas it presented and treated underwent a radical and revolutionary change.

Newtonian physics posited a continuous and mechanistic view of the universe in which time was conceived of as a series of separate points having duration. The novel of the nineteenth century recreated within itself this view of the universe and time. Consequently, in the nineteenth century narrative technique was appropriate to the predominant world view since it was intimately bound up with a specific concept of time which would permit no other formulation of time without the rejection of a mechanistic universe. Closely related to Newton's concepts of absolute time and absolute space was the "shape" he gave to the idea of cause. J. Bronoswki tells us that "Our conception of cause and effect," as formulated by Newton, is "that given a definite configuration of wholly material things, there will always follow upon it the same observable event.

If we repeat the configuration, we shall always get the same event following it" (p. 41). In the novel, consequently, character was moved "forward from moment to moment in a precise chronological sequence" and functioned according to the Newtonian concept of cause and effect.[15] This is not to say that movement backwards in time was impossible. Obviously, such novels as those by Defoe or Richardson are memories, reminiscences, or reflections. Narrators in novels by Defoe or Richardson present an account of remembered experiences. The principle of memory may be psychological, but it implicitly involves a linear concept of time in which the order of events has been reversed and then represented in accordance with a strict chronology as, for instance, in *Moll Flanders*. The point to make, though, is that in novels such as these, the act of memory is ordered in a strict, chronological (historical) sequence which presupposes a causal formulation for time: that is, one thing followed another in the novel because time was conceived of as a series of separate points, one following another, from a beginning to an end bounded at their extreme limits by the births and deaths of the novel's characters. The psychological state of the narrator with respect to time, whether first person or omniscient, could be explained, and was explained, in terms of this causal formulation. Though human nature might be inextricable from itself, the ways in which that nature could be presented were predictable, and they were predictable because the concept of time implicit in the narrator's act of telling his story limited the possibilities of his presentation. In later fiction this is not necessarily the case since our world view has changed and with that change has come an entirely different way of looking at and understanding causality, time, and the universe. It is true that in one sense the very nature of literary art will always presuppose a chronological presentation, but this presentation is not necessarily inherent in the structure of the novel and is related to the nature of our language and the way it is structured. However, what is important is the way in which narrative technique is handled that makes the distinctions drawn here crucial. In modern fiction, and specifically in the contemporary science-fiction novel, we may still have first person narration but the way in which it is handled, presented, and understood has radically altered, and that alteration is the result of a shift in how man conceives of and understands the physical universe. The very phrase *first person narration* hints at what is being suggested. It inherently posits a chronological development, a linear formulation. In later chapters when discussing recent developments in narrative technique I will use in place of *first person narration* the phrase *fictive I* or *eye* (or both). To recapitulate, the phrase itself—*first person narration*—implicitly names a certain type of narrative device which is bound and limited to a specific concept of time, which may be formulated in a rather mechanical way. In other words, the mechanics of time in the nineteenth-century novel seem to be the mechanics of Newton's physics. And, while the eighteenth-and nineteenth-century novelists may have employed the narrative technique of memory or reminiscence, this technique was used in a chronological manner as a structural device for recapitulating the events which were psychologically (or otherwise) meaningful to the narrator. Obviously, as Jerome Buckley points out in *The Triumph of Time,* other concepts of time existed—but these concepts of time related to the way in which the Victorians saw history, progress, and decadence while the scientist "still dealt in an objective linear time to be measured quantitatively."[16] The point to be made here is that the narrative technique of a novel should be appropriate to its implicit world view. If the narrative technique of a novel is inappropriate to the novel's world view, then, in our view, the novel's narrative technique violates that world view or its (the novel's) ideas and is flawed. After all, the art of the novel lies directly in proportion to its seductiveness, that is, in its credibility, and this in turn is a function, as Coleridge would put it, of the reader's "willing suspension of disbelief." Whether or not the novel treats "reality" is of little concern. What is of concern is that the novel be believable in its own terms. In this sense, the novel must have internal consistency. In the novel of the nineteenth-century type, the novel which Sartre and Robbe-Grillet criticize, consistency becomes a major factor of a conception of the universe as orderly, where all parts function according to plan. In brief, as someone once observed, fiction is the "art of lying agreeably."

What has been suggested to this point, perhaps, needs no justification. It would seem obvious, for instance, that the world view of Newton did have its effect on the narrative technique of the novel. What is less obvious, perhaps, is that character when presented in the nineteenth-century novel must always function in terms of a causal universe. This is what Sartre is driving at when he accuses Mauriac of ignoring the principle of relativity. But Sartre himself commits a minor error in his argument. The error is that if Mauriac *chooses* to write novels which are in keeping with a different conception of the universe, then, he may, although it dates him to do so. This in itself may be an arguable point to make since it assumes that the *value* of the novelist's art lies directly in his keeping abreast of the newer theories of reality. And, perhaps, there are other values of art, and other theories in which this type of argument would be foreign. Nevertheless, it would seem safe to assume, for the moment, that one standard or criterion that may be used to judge the credibility of any fictional system is the degree to which its narrative devices (techniques) are appropriate or inappropriate to the world view, both implicit and explicit, which exists in the novel.

At the beginning of this chapter Heisenberg was quoted on the need to "examine the foundations which form the presuppositions for every development of art, foundations which at other times are taken as self-evident." In his essay Heisenberg correctly argues that "it may be valuable for the artist to consider what changes have occurred during the last decade in the scientific view of nature." Further, Heisenberg's essay provides a convenient way of summing up in its broad outlines the major world views of the last three hundred years and their relevance to literary art. Consequently, like Heisenberg, I wish to examine the changes which have occurred in the scientific view of nature, for at the heart of this study stands the idea that the change in the way in which science views nature has resulted in a radical shift in the art of the science-fiction novel. Further, the "arguments" of the three central chapters of my book not only make use of this new view of nature but presuppose a basic knowledge and understanding of this view of nature and its relation to narrative technique. And, like Sartre, I will posit the idea that the narrative devices of fiction must be appropriate to the implicit world view that exists in the narrative and that, in part, our conception of fictional devices is shaped by this view and may be understood only by realizing its literary and philosophical implications.

Heisenberg begins his essay—"The Representation of Nature in Contemporary Physics"—by tracing the "historical roots of recent science" to the seventeenth century and Kepler:

> When this science was being established in the seventeenth century by Kepler, Galileo, and Newton, the medieval image was at first still unbroken: man saw in nature God's creation. Nature was thought of as the work of God. It would have seemed senseless to people of that time to ask about the material world apart from God. (p. 123)

In the decades which followed Kepler, however, it was seen that man's relation toward nature altered fundamentally. This alteration, in at least one sense, would become responsible for modern literary criticism since it was this change in man's relation with nature which gave science its impetus. Edgar Stanley Hyman in *The Armed Vision* suggests that the power of modern literary criticism derives essentially from the fact that it is an "organized use of nonliterary techniques and bodies of knowledge to obtain insights into literature" and that these bodies of knowledge are those of science.[17] And as Heisenberg points out, science followed "Galileo's example" and began "to separate out individual processes of nature from their environment, describe them mathematically, and thus 'explain' them" (p. 123). This process of separation broke the medieval image of nature, for it clearly presented science with the task of endless description. Heisenberg tells us that "Newton could no longer see the world as the work of God, comprehensible only as a whole. His position toward nature is most clearly circumscribed by his well-known statement that he felt like a child playing at the seashore, happy wherever he found a smoother pebble or a more beautiful sea shell than usual, while the great ocean of truth lay unexplored before him" (p. 123). It may be argued that in a limited sense the history of science has shown that science has been, since Newton's time, an attempt to regain the medieval view of nature comprehensible only as a whole. In other words, Newtonian thought led to a fragmentation of human knowledge. Integration of the way in which man saw the physical world would not be achieved again until Einstein. Nevertheless, this separation of God from nature and the growing tendency to describe the processes of nature mathematically, as Heisenberg suggests, "may perhaps be better understood when we consider that, to some Christian thought of the period, God in heaven seemed so far removed from earth that it became meaningful to view the earth apart from God. Thus there may even be justification in speaking of a specifically Christian form of godlessness in connection with modern science" (p. 123). One of the consequences of this tendency of science to separate nature from God and man found its final expression in the philosophy of Descartes, a separation which science has only overcome in this century. And as Heisenberg points out:

> It is certainly no coincidence that precisely in that period [Newton's], nature becomes the object of representation in the arts independent of religious themes. The same tendency comes to expression in science when nature is considered not only independent of God, but also independent of man, so that there is formed the ideal of an "objective" description or explanation of nature. Nevertheless, it must be emphasized that for Newton the sea shell is significant only because it comes from the great ocean of truth. Observing it is not yet an end in itself; rather, its study receives meaning through its relation to the whole. (p. 124)

The important thing which Heisenberg points out in this passage is the idea of observation. Observation has "not yet [become] an end in itself." This development will wait until the physics of the twentieth century to find its expression. As a result, then, of the widening influence of Newton's mechanics, technology became the key for obtaining information about those "remote regions of nature" which were unattainable otherwise (p. 124). "Thus," as Heisenberg suggests, "the meaning of the word 'nature' as an object of scientific research slowly changed; it became a collective concept for all those areas of experience into which man can penetrate through science and technology, whether or not they are given to him 'naturally' in direct experience" (p. 124). Further, the "term *de-*

scription of nature also progressively lost its original significance as a presentation intended to convey the most alive and imaginable picture possible of nature; instead, in increasing measure a mathematical description of nature was implied—that is, a collection of data concerning interrelations according to law in nature, precise and brief yet also as comprehensive as possible" (pp. 124–25). By the nineteenth century, however, "nature appeared as a lawful process in space and time, in whose description it was possible to ignore as far as axioms were concerned, even if not in practice, both man and his interference in nature (Heisenberg, p. 125). The consequences of this point of view of nature as a "lawful process" resulted in a world view which saw the physical universe as both orderly and continuous. Its significance, however, not only for science but for philosophy, was to give rise to the "familiar classification of the world into subject and object, inner and outer world, body and soul" (Heisenberg, p. 131). Nature in the eighteenth and first half of the nineteenth century, then, became increasingly lawful and gave rise to materialism. According to Heisenberg, materialism derives essentially from "the atomistic hypothesis taken over from antiquity" in which atoms became the "truly real" and "unchangeable building stones of matter" (p. 125). And, as Heisenberg points out:

> In the philosophy of Democritus, sensual qualities of matter were taken as appearance; smell and color, temperature and toughness were not intrinsic properties of matter, but originated as interactions between matter and our senses and thus had to be explained through the arrangement and motion of the atoms and the effects of this arrangement on our senses. In this way the all-too-simple world view of nineteenth-century materialism was formed: the atoms, as intrinsically unchangeable beings, move in space and time and, through their mutual arrangement and motion, call forth the colorful phenomena of our sense world. (p. 125)

The first "inroad into this simple world picture . . . occurred in the second half of the last century through the development of electrical theory in which not matter but rather the force field had to be taken as intrinsically real" (p. 125). It is, perhaps, unnecessary to trace the other inroads that appeared in the Newtonian world view or to become involved with their inner arguments. Rather, it is sufficient to say that inroads began to be made but did not seriously alter "the coherent world view of the nineteenth and early twentieth centuries" (p. 126). Yet it is at this point—with the appearance of the force field and the recognition that protons, neutrons, and electrons replaced the atom as the smallest building blocks of matter—that "profound changes in the foundations of atomic physics occurred in our century which . . . [led] away from the reality concept of classical atomism" (Heisenberg, p. 126). Heisenberg declares that "It has turned out that the hoped-for objective reality of the elementary particles [protons, neutrons, and electrons] represents too rough a simplification of the true state of affairs and must yield to much more abstract conceptions" (p. 126). He continues:

> When we wish to picture to ourselves the nature of the existence of the elementary particles, we may no longer ignore the physical process by which we obtain information about them. When we are observing objects of our daily experience, the physical process transmitting the observation of course plays only a secondary role. However, for the smallest building blocks of matter every process of observation causes a major disturbance; it turns out that we can no longer talk of the behavior of the particle apart from the process of observation. In consequence, we are finally led to believe that the laws of nature which we formulate mathematically in quantum theory deal no longer with the particles themselves but with our knowledge of the elementary particles. (pp. 126-27)

With this fundamental recognition and understanding of the role that observation plays in our perception of elementary particles comes a different world view. Where Newtonian mechanics separated nature from man and God and rendered itself to "objectification," modern science reintegrates man with nature through a recognition of the significance of observation, but it does so in a way radically different from that of previous ages. The essential distinctions between the world view of Newton and that of our current situation are nicely stated by Heisenberg who points out that "When we speak of a picture of nature provided by contemporary exact science, we do not actually mean any longer a picture of nature, but rather a picture of our relation to nature" (p. 134). Further, the "old compartmentalization of the world into an objective process in space and time, on the one hand, and the soul in which this process is mirrored," as Heisenberg notes, "on the other—that is, the Cartesian differentiation of *res cognitans* and *res extensa*—is no longer suitable as the starting point for the understanding of modern science" (p. 134). Heisenberg suggests that:

> In the field of view of this science [modern science] there appears above all the network of relations between man and nature of the connections through which we as physical beings are dependent parts of nature and at the same time, as human beings, make them the object of our thought and actions. Science no longer is in the position of observer of nature, but recognizes itself as part of the interplay between man and nature. The scientific method of separating, explaining, and arranging becomes conscious of its limits, set by the fact that the employment of this procedure can no longer keep its distance from the object. The world view of natural science thus ceases to be a view of "natural" science in its proper sense. (p. 134)

Where the novel of the eighteenth and nineteenth century presented a picture of nature, that is, its metaphors were drawn from nature and presented a picture of nature, the modern novel, the novel of the twentieth century, presents us with a series of metaphors which "picture . . . our relation to nature." The distinction between these two ways of "structuring" the novel is crucial, because each, after its own fashion, creates an implicit world view in the novel and, in turn, is created by that world view. The structural basis of contemporary science-fiction novels, such as *The Einstein Intersection, Report on Probability A,* and *Slaughterhouse-Five,* results, not from a series of metaphors taken directly from nature, but is derived essentially from modern mathematical physics. In other words, something stands intermediately as a model (rather than as a set of metaphors) between nature and its representation in the novel. In the case of *The Einstein Intersection,* this something is the theory of relativity, the principles of which are reflected in the structure of the novel and are worked out in terms of their implications for the narrative technique of the novel. The implicit world view of *Report on Probability A* is based specifically on probability theory and the Principle of Uncertainty. *Slaughterhouse-Five,* though a somewhat more traditional title than *The Einstein Intersection* or *Report on Probability A,* reflects the Einsteinian concept of space-time. What is being suggested, then, is that the foundations of the novel, like those of science itself, have undergone a shift in their structure and that this shift in turn brings about a change in their form and the way in which we understand the nature of form. For these novels present a picture of man's *relation* to nature, rather than a picture *of* nature from which man is absent. Representation per se, then becomes a moot question and, as Booth points out:

> A dialectical history of modern criticism could be written in terms of the warfare between those who think of fiction as something that must above all be real . . . and those who ask that it be pure—even if the search for artistic purity should lead to unreality and a "dehumanization of art." (p. 38)

Booth's formulation of this conflict between what must be "real" and what is "pure," however, is dependent on how we perceive and conceive of nature. In the view of modern science, and the incorporation of that view into the structure of the modern novel, this problem becomes entirely academic and, depending upon one's point of view, may disappear entirely. Science fiction, and specifically the three novels to be treated here, do not lend themselves to a representational theory of art. The reason for this is, in part, simple enough. Science fiction makes the claim to treat a nonexistent reality, an imaginative reality which may have its origins in our own reality but which, because it usually extrapolates a future not yet existent, cannot represent our reality but only its own. In other words, to borrow a phrase from Robbe-Grillet, the novel "*constitutes* reality" and what "it explores is itself" (pp. 160–61). Yet in the novel's exploration of itself what we shall discover is that the principles which give rise to the novel and which exist within it are based on "a description of the world or, better, a language for describing the world" and that this language is science and its principles (Bronowski, p. 48). Consequently, it is only by rather remote and indirect means that we may speak of these novels as being representational. Robbe-Grillet suggests that:

> The best possible method is still to extrapolate, and this is precisely what vital criticism attempts to do. Taking as its foundation the historical evolution of forms and of their significations, in the Western novel, for example, criticism can attempt to imagine what tomorrow's significations will be, and then to offer a provisional judgment as to the forms the artist affords it today. (p. 144)

In discussing the relation between narrative technique and the world view in this chapter, I have laid the foundations for a distinction between the historical forms of the novel, and those which currently exist in the science-fiction novel. In the chapters which follow I shall explore the ways in which the world view of modern mathematical physics influences the narrative technique of three contemporary science-fiction novels.

2

Relativity and the Universe of Fiction

> *And when his friend Janos Plesh commented years later that there seemed to be some connection between mathematics and fiction, a field in which the writer made a world out of invented characters and situations and then compared it with the existing world Einstein replied: "There may be something in what you say. When I examine myself and my methods of thought I come to the conclusion that the gift of fantasy has meant more to me than my talent for absorbing positive knowledge."*
>
> Ronald W. Clark, *Einstein: The Life and Times*

In this chapter I will examine what seems to be a connection between the invented worlds of mathematical physics and fiction in terms of Samuel R. Delany's *The Einstein Intersection*.[1] It is my belief that a relationship exists between these two worlds and that *The Einstein Intersection* is a literary expression of that relationship. I am not, however, making some special claim for science fiction. I am only pointing out that science fiction is a type of literature and, as such, that it must be initially judged by the standards of that literature. It should be remembered, then, that there is nothing inherently difficult in understanding the relationship that exists between mathematical physics and fiction as long as we recognize that *The Einstein Intersection*, like any literary work of art, "is governed by precisely the same literary and dramatic requirements as any other form of literature."[2] The problem, insofar as it may be a problem, resides in the form of the novel. Alain Robbe-Grillet points out that "A new form will always seem more or less an absence of any form at all, since it is unconsciously judged by reference to the consecrated forms."[3] Essentially, the problems of *The Einstein Intersection* are related to the problems of form. Since most of what will be discussed here relates directly or indirectly to form, it would seem wise tentatively to define what is meant by that term. Yet definition itself seems somehow inadequate to deal with the problems of form since, as Charles W. Misner points out in *Gravitation*:

> In science, as stressed not least by Henri Poincaré, that view is out of date which used to say, "Define your terms before you proceed." All the laws and theories of physics . . . have this deep and subtle character, that they both define the concepts they use . . . and make statements about these concepts. Contrariwise, the absence of some body of theory, law, and principle deprives one of the means properly to define or even use concepts. Any forward step in human knowledge is truly creative in this sense: that theory, concept, law, and method of measurement—forever inseparable—are born into the world in union.[4]

Misner's view of the problem of definition in science constitutes a functional or operational definition of terminology. What is true for science is, perhaps, even more appropriate for the study of literature. Our critical vocabulary is woefully inadequate and our definition of the rather limited critical terms we do have, such as those found in Wayne C. Booth's *The Rhetoric of Fiction* and other works concerned with the long narrative, are often wanting with respect to precision. Nevertheless, for the purpose of exigency, I shall use Charles Olson's definition of form, that is, "FORM IS NEVER MORE THAN AN EXTENSION OF CONTENT" as a starting point.[5] What is being suggested is that the forms a novel may take grow out of the ideas and concepts, both implicit and explicit, which reside in it. Form and content are not antithetical concepts. Rather, form expresses an "extension" of certain ideas and concepts which, because of their particular expression, find themselves arranged in a particular pattern or relationship. This pattern or relationship we call a novel.

In brief, Delany has invented, quite freely, a new form for the science-fiction novel. In *The Einstein Intersection,* the traditional divisions of the novel into separate and clearly-discernible chapters are gone, and in their place the narration is briefly interrupted by quotations from the author's journal, quotations from various literary, religious, philosophical, and scientific sources, and quotations from other fictional works of art. These quotations serve an important function in the structure of the novel since they provide a series of points that force the reader to relate the story to his own time. For instance, at the beginning of the second section of the novel Delany provides a rather lengthy description of his impressions of a week's stay in Venice and relates this stay to his problems in "trying the assimilate . . . Lobey's [the main character of the novel] adventure," though he admits that he doesn't "quite know how" these problems of assimilation will be worked out (pp. 13–14). In other words, as Delany attempts to relate Lobey's story to his own time, we too, analogically, must relate Delany's experiences to our own. Delany in this particular section (and in others like it from his journal) attempts to establish a sense of aesthetic distance between the story the novel presents (it takes place in the distant future when man has left his planet and gone elsewhere in the universe) and the historical present. This relationship between the story the novel presents and the historical present is paralleled within the novel by the presence of a series of allusions and images that establish a continuity in time between the distant historical past when man still inhabited the earth, the immediate historical past which presents the narrator's own history and his knowledge of his race's history, the present, and the future. There is, perhaps, another and more important function these quotations serve and this function is intimately related to the form of the novel; that is, the quotations allow us to observe, in a limited sense, the author's view of how he understands the creative process and its relation to Lobey's story and *The Einstein Intersection*. For example, in a quotation from the author's journal at the beginning of section twelve, Delany informs us that "In a week another birthday, and I can start the meticulous process of overlaying another filigree across the novel's palimpsest" (p. 137). What Delany has presented is a description of the way in which he understands the process of his creation of the novel. Further, the relationship that exists in the novel between mathematical physics and fiction is relatively complex since it involves an understanding of certain key concepts in contemporary physics. These concepts are presented within the novel, and an understanding of their presence is crucial to any discussion of it. It would seem sensible, therefore, to examine what Martin Dyck in "Relativity in Physics and in Fiction" terms "some striking analogies" that exist "between physics and fiction," since I am dealing with the nature of fiction and, specifically, its relationship to physics and the world view implicit in *The Einstein Intersection*.[6] For it is only through coming to terms with the form of *The Einstein Intersection* that we may come to understand the relationship between the invented worlds of mathematics and fiction in the novel.

James B. Conant tells us that the mathematician or physicist "no longer pretends that he is dealing with reality, but accepts instead that he works with interlocking conceptual schemes—with models—that are productive for a time but are constantly modified."[7] Further, it may be argued that "Few, if any writers would now insist that their fictional worlds reproduce reality. Instead the writer creates a model, an imitation, a symbolic construct through which he tries to capture the quality of human experience."[8] Since neither the physicist nor the writer pretends any longer that he is dealing with reality, the models he creates in his attempts to render the world intelligible may seem to be nothing more than a series of metaphors. These metaphors, however, are not taken from nature but have their source in the abstract principles of science.

Martin Dyck in his essay suggests that "In a basic sense, both fiction and physics are physics" (p. 174). Dyck's formulation about the analogical similarities between physics and fiction strikes to the center of a particular twentieth-century problem in epistemology and ontology. The problem is not simply a matter of defining what we mean by fiction and physics. It involves what Thomas S. Kuhn in *The Structure of Scientific Revolutions* terms "incommensurable ways of seeing the world and of practicing science in it."[9] Further, it might be added, it involves a switch or change in the way in which the artist sees his function or purpose in his art and, therefore, in his world. Kuhn points out that "What a man sees depends both upon what he looks at and also upon what his previous visual-conceptual experience has taught him to see. In the absence of such training there can only be, in William James' phrase, "a bloomin' buzzin' confusion" (p. 113). The question which Dyck raises is "In what sense is physics fiction?" and declares, "Well, what else is it? Truth? A physicist would object to such classification. Reality? Past the mid-twentieth century we are no longer so naive as to assume that there is such a thing as a definable reality" (p. 11). The reasons for this are not simple and involve the theory of relativity. Lincoln Barnett argues that "the irony of man's quest for reality is that as nature is stripped of its disguises, as order emerges from chaos and unity from diversity, as concepts merge and fundamental laws assume increasingly simpler form, the evolving picture becomes ever more remote from experience—far stranger indeed and less recognizable than the bone structure behind a familiar face."[10] Reality in modern physics ceases to be a meaningful concept. Barnett notes that:

> In trying to distinguish appearance from reality and lay bare the fundamental structure of the universe, science has had to transcend the "rabble of the senses." But its highest edifices, Einstein has pointed out, have been "purchased at the price of emptiness of content." A theoretical concept is emptied of content to the very degree that it is divorced from sensory experience. For the only world man can truly know is the world created for him by the senses. (pp. 113–14)

Barnett argues that "in the abstract lexicon of quantum physics there is no such word as 'really' " (p. 32). Further, he suggests that "The certainty that science can explain *how* things happen began to dim about twenty years ago. And right now it is a question whether scientific man is in touch with 'reality' at all—or can ever hope to be" (p. 16). According to Barnett, the theory of relativity does not "contradict classical physics. It simply regards the old concepts as limiting cases that apply solely to the familiar experiences of man" (p. 58). Consequently, as he suggests, "Einstein thus surmounts the barrier reared by man's impulse to define reality solely as he perceives it through the screen of his senses" (p. 58). He further comments that:

> The world of light and color, of blue skies and green leaves, of sighing wind . . . the world designed by the physiology of human sense organs—is the world in which finite man is incarcerated by his essential nature. And what the scientist and the philosopher call the world of reality—the colorless, soundless, impalpable cosmos which lies like an iceberg beneath the plane of man's perceptions—is a skeleton structure of symbols.
> And the symbols change. (p. 114)

In *The Einstein Intersection,* for instance, Lobey's perception of his world is essentially stable and coherent. What he perceives is limited to the world presented by his senses. His familiar experiences may be unusual and odd for us, but in his world they are normal. In other words, Lobey is unaware of what the philosopher would call the world of reality. What he perceives as normal—he describes himself as "ugly and grinning most of the time" and as having "a figure like a bowling pin, thighs, calves, and feet of a man (gorilla?) twice my size (which is about five-nine) and hips to match"—is clearly unusual for us (pp. 5–6). Though Lobey's perception of his world is "innocent," our perception of his universe differs markedly from his. By the end of the novel, however, everything has become different; that is, Lobey no longer perceives a fixed and stable universe. He has come to understand what Doric tells him early in section four, that "this is the real world you're living in. It's come from something; it's going to something; it's changing" (p. 53). He understands not only the nature of change but the role it plays in his world and in his perception of that world, so much so that the only thing that is predictable is change itself. The novel grows out of the narrator's way of seeing his world come into conflict with his actual experience of it. The central conflict or paradox thus created grows out of the fact that what a man may "truly know" is limited by his senses to his familiar experience, while, at the same time, his science informs him that his senses are but imperfect instruments that lack the power and refinement to perceive the immeasurably small but significant events in the physical world that exist outside the range of his senses. While science, as Barnett points out, tells us "nothing of the true 'nature' of things, it nevertheless succeeds in defining their relationships and depicting the events in which they are involved. 'The event,' Alfred North Whitehead declared, 'is the unit of things real' " (p. 110). Science may tell us "nothing of the true 'nature' of things," but its "skeleton structure of symbols," does influence and produce a change in the way in which man sees the world.

Kuhn notes in Chapter X ("Revolutions as Changes of World View") that "the assimilation of a previously anomalous visual field has reacted upon and changed the field itself" (p. 112). If we substitute the term "visual-conceptual" for the purely "visual" in Kuhn's sentence, then we come close to describing the relation that exists between mathematical physics and fiction in the novel and its relationship to the narrator's way of seeing in his world. Because, in a sense, the literary significance of the theory of relativity is that it allows man, in the final analysis, to see himself, as Barnett states, "merely [as] an ephemeral conformation of the primordial space-time field. Man stands 'midway between macrocosm and microcosm' " and "finds barriers on every side and can perhaps but marvel, as St. Paul did nineteen hundred years ago, that 'the world was created by the word of God so that what is seen was made out of things which did not appear' " (p. 118). The theory of relativity points toward another significant development in modern physics.

J. Bronowski in *The Common Sense of Science* points out that Werner Heisenberg's *Gedankenexperimente* (the term means literally "thought experiments") showed "that every description of nature contains some essential and irremovable uncertainty. For example, the more accurately we try to measure the position of a fundamental particle, of an electron, say, the less certain will we be of its speed. The more accurately we try to estimate its speed, the more uncertain will we be of its precise position."[11] Further, as Barnett notes, in "the very act of observing its position [the electron's], its velocity is changed; and, conversely, the more accurately its velocity is determined, the more indefinite its position becomes" (p. 34). The significance of Heisenberg's Principle of Uncertainty was not missed by philosophers or artists. Plato had argued that "The prison house is the world of sight," and, as Barnett and others have pointed out, "Every seeming avenue of escape from this prison house that science has surveyed leads only deeper into a misty realm of symbolism and abstraction" (p. 116). Barnett further argues that "it may be that the extreme and insurmountable limit of scientific knowledge will be reached in the attainment of perfect isomorphic representation—that is, in a final flawless concurrence of theory and natural process, so complete that every observed phenomena is accounted for and nothing is left out of the picture" (p. 116). The same speculation may be made for the limits of literary art and theory where the literary artist continually strives to create a perfect and final flawless account of human nature. This, of course, he must accomplish within the limitations imposed upon him by his senses while at the same time he takes into account new understandings of the universe revealed to him by his science. As Robbe-Grillet puts it, "Obviously I am concerned, in any case, only with the world as *my point of view* orients it; I shall never know any other. The relative sense of sight serves me precisely to define *my situation in the world*. I simply keep myself from helping to make this situation a servitude."[12] In a sense, this is exactly the narrator's position in *The Einstein Intersection*. The point to be made here is that reality conceived of as an "absolute" ceases to be a meaningful concept in modern science. Dyck declares:

> More accurately; there is no *one* definable truth or reality. And since there is more than one conception of truth and reality, to any *one* observer all but his own conception of truth and reality must be fictitious. And since we cannot be so subjective as to accept the truth and reality of any one individual, or one group, or one society, or one branch of knowledge, or one age as truth and reality binding on all and always binding (though we do not deny any individual, or group, or age the bliss of pursuing his or its own fictions) we are forced to conclude that all concepts of truth and reality are fictitious. (p. 174)

The conclusion Dyck reaches seems valid enough and, in a limited sense, *The Einstein Intersection* represents the attempt of one individual (Lo Lobey) to pursue his own fictions only to discover in the search (quest) that his concepts of truth and reality, of the nature of his world, are fictitious. Delany quotes Jean-Paul Sartre at the beginning of the fifth section of the novel to the effect that "Experience reveals to him in every object, in every event, the presence of something else" (p. 55). Earlier in the novel Doric, the "kage-keeper," tells Lobey "this is the real world you're living in. It's come from something; it's going to something; it's changing. But it's got right and wrong, a way to behave and a way not to. You never wanted to accept that, even when you were a kid, but until you do, you won't be very happy" (p. 53). Lobey's unwillingness to accept the nature of his world is in part a failure of his willingness to *see* his world. He staggers through this "abstracted novel," pursuing, like the author Delany, his own fictions (p. 118). Delany tells us at the beginning of section two that "It turned windy as we floated beneath the black wood arch of the Ponti Academia; I was trying to assimilate the flowers, the vicious animals, with Lobey's adventure—each applies, but as yet I don't quite know how" (p. 13). The information Delany's journal supplies suggests that he wishes to make a close analogy between the writer's pursuit of his own fictions and those fictions pursued by his major character.

Someone may object, however, to what has been suggested about the nature of physics and argue that "physics" should be described "as physical reality, or a set of theories of physical reality, or of the physical universe" and, therefore, should not be compared with literary works of art (Dyck, p. 174). The apparent reason for this objection is that literary art is a product of the mind and is concerned with human experience whereas physics is concerned with the physical world only. The resulting argument holds that physics and literary art are incommensurate since they deal with radically divergent phenomena. Obviously nothing could be further from the truth, as I have already partly shown. As Dyck points out, if physics should be considered in terms of one of these propositions, or all, then, each "of these propositions holds true. And each is circular. And each is incomplete" (p. 174). In what ways are these "propositions" circular and incomplete? What is missing? I have already suggested that contemporary physics no longer deals with reality but with realities and that an event cannot be separated from a fact and an observation, that the two are mutually related and tied together in an observation and that the very act of observation itself produces or causes a change in the thing observed. Dyck suggests:

> Each leaves out myriads of qualities and iridescences that impinge, physically, on the human senses and the imagination. If a physicist should object by saying that what his systems and theories leave out is due to his science not having caught up with all phenomena he would confirm hitherto established physics as fictitious because new insights will lead to modified fiction and a clearer realization of the fictitiousness of current physics. If he should object by surmising that man will *never* entirely grasp nature's mysteries he would in so surmising proclaim that man's physics must always remain fiction. And his hunches about the unexplored might be classified as unpublished fiction—unless, of course, he is a cosmologist. But to be a cosmologist is to be a poet. Man cannot exist in the void. He needs a solid footing in the universe. And what could be more solid than fiction? (p. 174)

If physics is a type of fiction and *The Einstein Intersection* is an imaginative invention, a fiction, then at what point or points do the fictions of mathematical physics and fiction intersect in the novel? In one sense this seems to be the central concern and question of Delany's novel; isn't it implicit in the title itself? After all, *The Einstein Intersection* suggests that something intersects with something else and that the novel is a representation of that intersection. In other words, the title of the novel "names" or delineates something that takes place in the novel—an event, an occurrence—between the creative act and the imagination and the way in which the narrator perceives his world. For the world created in the novel, and presented by the novel, is going to rest, in the final analysis, on the particular understanding the narrator holds of the nature of his experience and the physical world. This in turn will be dependent upon how the narrator reveals his world, that is, the narrative strategy and technique of the novel. The answer to the question, "At what point or points do the fictions of mathematical physics and fiction intersect?" resides in the form of the novel. For form, in the sense that I am using it here, becomes a synonym for model. Yet a model is a system which not only defines itself but something else, and that something else is nothing less than the novel.

So far I have discussed the relationship that exists between mathematical physics and fiction and suggested their similarities. However, it is clear that fiction, that is, the novel, may in its own right present a picture of its world and, therefore, present indirectly a physics. The concepts Lobey holds shape the way in which he sees his world while his experience of that world forces him to reshape his fundamental ideas about its nature. In other words, the novel considered as a fictional system, or model, will force us to examine the narrator's own particular conceptions and realizations (creative or otherwise) of *his* world. Yet the way in which the narrator sees his world will take shape and form out of the intersection of physics with fiction in his own mind. This, after its own fashion, presents certain problems. Witold Gombrowicz suggests, "Man is made in such a way that he continually has to define himself and continually escape his own definitions. Reality is not about to let itself be completely enclosed in form. Form for its part does not agree with the essence of life. Yet all thought that tries to define the inadequacy of form becomes form in its own turn and thus only confirms our tendency towards form."[13]

Delany tells us that "the central subject of the book is myth" (p. 78). But the novel is not concerned with specific myths per se, such as Orpheus, or as Stephen Scobie speculates, with Norse mythology. Rather, the novel is concerned with "why we have them," as Delany informs us, that is, myths, and "what we use them for" (p. 126). *The Einstein Intersection* is set in the distant future, long after the holocaust of nuclear war (post-deluge or after the flood is its archetypal counterpart) has destroyed most of the planet. Lobey, the narrator of the story, is in love with a girl named Friza. They are not human. They have inherited man's "bodies, their souls—both husks abandoned here for any wanderer's taking," as Spider (sidekick and seer) informs us (p. 129). Friza is killed by Kid Death (symbolized in the novel by Billy the Kid). Lobey (Orpheus?) must set out on a quest to find Friza and regain her. Early in the novel Lobey falls into the ruins of an abandoned maze of underground shelters. He faces and kills a futuristic minotaur. He confronts a machine, and as he tells us, "It was a computer from the old time (when you owned this Earth, you wraiths and memories), a few of which chuckled and chattered throughout the source-cave. I'd had them described to me, but this was

28 Relativity and Fiction

the first I'd seen" (p. 34). The computer's name is "PHAEDRA." In the conversation that takes place between Lobey and Phaedra we learn from Phaedra that she was placed in the underground complex "by people who never dreamed that you would come. Psychic Harmony Entanglements and Deranged Response Association, that was my department. And you've come down here hunting through my memories for your lost girl" (p. 38). Lobey's quest for Friza, however, is difficult. He must somehow find his way out of the maze—the objective correlative to mankind's "million year old fantasies" (p. 39). Phaedra tells Lobey "You're basically not equipped for it. . . . But I suppose you have to exhaust the old mazes before you can move into the new ones. It's hard" (p. 39). Lobey sometime later, after finding his way out of the maze, joins a dragon drive (cattle drive?) on its way to Branning-at-sea (Dodge City?). He meets Spider and Green-eye. They arrive at Branning-at-sea; with Spider's help, Billy the Kid is killed, Green-eye (Christ?) is crucified and hung from a tree, and Lobey meets the Dove. Near the end of the novel Spider explains to Lobey:

> As we are able to retain more and more of our past, it takes us longer and longer to become old; Lobey, everything changes. The Labyrinth today does not follow the same path it did at Knossos fifty thousand years ago. You may be Orpheus; you may be someone else, who dares death and succeeds. Green-eye may go to the tree this evening, hang there, rot, and never come down. The world is not the same. That's what I've been trying to tell you. It's different. (p. 131)

Delany has informed us earlier in the novel that "Endings to be useful must be inconclusive" (p. 137). Lobey's search for Friza becomes a quest for his own identity. He must leave the earth and go, like man, to the stars. Lobey explains "In my village there was a man who grew dissatisfied. So he left this world, worked for a while on the moon, on the outer planets, then on worlds that were stars away. I might go there" (p. 155). Spider, in reply to Lobey's statement, declares "I did that once. It was all waiting for me when I got back" (p. 155). Lobey, however, wishes to know "What's it going to be like?" and Spider suggests "It's not going to be what you expect" (p. 155). Lobey hesitantly questions "It's going to be . . . different?" (p. 155). And, of course, the answer to this question is the conclusion of the novel—and that conclusion is inconclusive. The novel ends with Lobey telling us "As morning branded the sea, darkness fell away at the far side of the beach. I turned to follow it" (p. 155). In a sense Lobey's journey has already been taken since he has told us his story, that is, conceptually, the end of the novel is its beginning and vice versa.

It was suggested earlier that something intersects with something else in the novel and that this intersection becomes the novel, that is, *The*

Einstein Intersection. The Einsteinian world of relativity *intersects* with the Goedelian to reveal, at that point of intersection, the limitations and possibilities of human activity. Intersection, as used here, is used in its mathematical sense—as a conjunction of two or more sets of objects whose elements are mutually shared by both in the same area. In the novel there exists a set of ideas which are given expression by Spider to Lobey about the nature of his world. These ideas are taken from mathematical physics. In addition to these ideas there exists a set of ideas which are concerned with the nature of the creative act, the creative process, and the life of the imagination. These ideas, that is, the ideas concerned with the nature of creativity, are often expressed by Delany in quotations from his journal which are prefixed to the beginning of various sections of the novel. However, these ideas, like the ones from mathematical physics, are also expressed by various characters in the novel and are reflected in the form and structure of the novel. It is out of the intersection of these two sets of ideas that the form of the novel grows. Further, the intersection of these two basic sets of ideas defines the starting and stopping points of the novel.

Few readers will be without some knowledge of Einstein and the theory of relativity, part of which I have already explored in terms of physics, while other readers will know little about Kurt Goedel. Howard DeLong in discussing the implications of Goedel's proof in "Unsolved Problems in Arithmetic" explains that:

> The central change that the limitative theorems [of Goedel] required of all previous theories of the nature of mathematics was the recognition that there are unanswerable questions in the subject. Earlier it had been thought that if a question could be made precise, that question had an answer. Now it was seen that perhaps some precise questions do not have precise answers. By way of analogy, think of an object, say a light bulb. If you then ask, "Is it made partly of cork?" the answer will probably be no. If, however, you ask, "Does it weigh exactly 3.1 ounces?" the question is probably unanswerable. The reality toward which the question is directed is indeterminate in some ways. Such indeterminateness is characteristic of products of the imagination, including artistic creations. ("How often did Juliet sneeze during the year before she met Romeo?") In these areas it is pointless to ask questions about things that are not determined by evidence.
> Compared with imaginative creations, physical reality is determinate, and yet, the results of quantum theory suggest that physical reality is also indeterminate in certain ways.[14]

Here we have a type of indirect statement about the indeterminate nature of imaginative creations. What is clear, or should be clear, is that there are essentially a set of unanswerable questions about the subject of literary art. For instance, there exists a set of precise questions I may ask about *The Einstein Intersection* which are unanswerable. I might ask "How old is Lobey?" and there is nothing in the novel which will allow me to answer this question precisely. Lobey's age is not given. All I may answer is that Lobey seems, from the various descriptions he gives of himself, to be relatively young. What the limitation theorems "represent," then, "is the discovery of an abstract structure for which it is impossible for any human being to make systematically complete and correct assumptions about" (DeLong, p. 59). It may also be pointed out that "Our powers of conceptual discrimination have limits just as our powers of perceptual discrimination do" (DeLong, p. 59).

As DeLong explains, Goedel's incompleteness theorem:

> states (roughly) that for any known formal systems for arithmetic there are formal sentences analogous to P, that is, either the system is incorrect (proves falsehoods) or it is incomplete (contains truths not provable in the system). 'P' stands for the sentence "This sentence is not provable".... The existence of P does not make the system inconsistent, but it does produce something disconcerting: P is true if and only if P is not provable. Hence we conclude that if we have P, then the cozy relation between truth and provability that one attempts to achieve in a formal system, namely that the set of sentences true under any interpretation that makes the axioms true be identical with the set of provable sentences, is destroyed. The liar has disappeared but his grin, like the Cheshire cat's, remains behind. (p. 56)

DeLong is referring to the "liar paradox" formulated by the ancient Greeks which can be stated, as he suggests, as "the problem of deciding whether or not the following sentence is true: 'This sentence is not true' " (p. 56). For obvious reasons, it is all but impossible to outline the general idea of Goedel's proof in more than a brief fashion here, and, as DeLong points out, all we can hope to convey is the "spirit of the proof" (p. 56). Philosophically, what is significant for the student of literature is that Goedel's proof suggests that there may be (from a mathematician's point of view, indeed, are) limitations to man's abilities. This may be stated another way by suggesting that any critical reading of a literary work of art which presupposes to examine a novel, for instance, only in terms of what is contained in the novel, will fail. In other words, in theory, the assumption that critical presuppositions about the nature of literary art may be proved by relying completely upon internal evidence is impossible without stepping outside that system (the literary work of art). Further, it may be argued that the novel must be open-ended and contain assertions, ideas and concepts which will not be provable by relying on that which is given in the novel itself. In summary, where Goedel's proof establishes, for the mathematician, the idea that there *are* limitations to man's abilities, so too, in the novel, Spider's explanation of the nature of the world of Lobey establishes the limitations of his world and his position in it.

Delany begins section eleven of *The Einstein Intersection* with three quotations, one from *The Revelation of John,* an excerpt from a letter from James Agee to Father Flye, and a short passage from Plotinus' *Enneads.* Each of these quotations, in its own way, points toward the significance of this section as the center of the novel—artistically, philosophically, and conceptually.

> *But I have this against thee, that thou didst leave thy first love.*
>
> The Revelation of John, Chapter 2, verse 4

> *My trouble is, such a subject cannot be seriously looked at without intensifying itself toward a center which is beyond what I, or anyone else, is capable of writing of . . . Trying to write it in terms of moral problems alone is more than I can possibly do. My main hope is to state the central subject and my ignorance from the start.*
>
> James Agee, *Letter to Father Flye*

> *Where is this country? How does one get there? If one is a born lover with an innate philosophic bent, one will get there.*
> Plotinus, *The Intelligence, the Idea and Being*

After wandering about Branning-at-sea for some time Lobey finds himself at Spider's house. Ostensibly, Lobey has gone to Spider's home to collect his pay. Spider asks Lobey to sit down, "I want to talk to you" (p. 125). Lobey answers, " 'About what' . . . Our voices echoed. The music was nearly silent. 'I have to be on my way to get Friza, to find Kid Death' " (p. 126). Spider tells Lobey, "That's why I suggest you sit down. . . . What do you know about mythology, Lobey?" (p. 126). Lobey recounts briefly his meager knowledge of mythology to Spider and Spider once again questions, "Again, what do you know about mythology?— I'm not asking you what myths we have, nor even where they come from, but why we have them, what we use them for" (p. 126). Lobey initially believes that the function of mythology is to guide him in his search for Friza. He tells us, "I could offer nothing else" (p. 126). Spider then raises the central question which leads to the center of this section and the novel "Do you understand difference, Lobey?" (p. 127). Lobey replies, "I live in a different world, where many have it [difference] and many do not.

I just discovered it myself weeks ago. I know the world moves toward it with every pulse of the great rock and the great roll. But I don't understand it" (p. 127). We are briefly told that all we can ever hope to know of difference "is what it is not" (p. 127). Spider, in answer to Lobey's "What isn't it?" replies in a rather lengthy explanation that:

> It isn't telepathy; it's not telekinesis—though both are chance phenomena that increase as difference increases. Lobey, Earth, the world, fifth planet from the sun—the species that stands on two legs and roams this thin wet crust: it's changing, Lobey. It's not the same. Some people walk under the sun and accept that change, others close their eyes, clap their hands to their ears and deny the world with their tongues. Most snicker, giggle, jeer and point when they think no one else is looking—that is how the humans acted throughout their history. We have taken over their abandoned world, and something new is happening to the fragments, something we can't define with mankind's leftover vocabulary. You must take its importance exactly as that: it is wonderful, fearful, deep, ineffable to your explanations, opaque to your efforts to see through it; yet it demands you take journeys, defines your stopping and starting points, can propel you with love and hate, even to seek death for Kid Death. . . . (p. 127)

Lobey finishes Spider's explanation with "— or make me make music . . ." even though he is unaware of the significance of what he has just suggested by his own conclusion (p. 127). Clearly, Lobey has not yet fully understood Spider. He questions, "What are you talking about Spider?" and Spider replies:

> If I could tell you, or you could understand from my inferences, Lobey, it would lose all value. Wars and chaoses and paradoxes ago, two mathematicians between them ended an age and began another for our hosts, our ghosts called Man. One was Einstein, who with his Theory of Relativity defined the limits of man's perception by expressing mathematically just how far the condition of the observer influences the thing he perceives. (pp. 127–28)

What Spider is trying to explain to Lobey is that man is a prisoner trapped by his senses in a world which he can only imperfectly understand. Yet the attempt must be made to come to an understanding of the essential nature of the world and man's position in it. As Spider has already explained, "it demands you take journeys," for it is only through defining "your stopping and starting points" that you may become aware of your own identity and your place in the world (p. 127). Once the nature of the world is discovered and understood it will open itself to the possibilities of creativity and change. We have already discussed at some length the significance of relativity and the limitations it imposes on the observer and the influence the observer may have on the thing he perceives. What is more important, however, is that the explanation Spider gives Lobey forms the nexus or analogical center and counterpart conceptually to the novel itself. Another way of stating this is to suggest that the novel is a fictional system which contains within itself its own explanation, this explanation containing, in a sense, the conceptual model of the novel. It clearly suggests what the function of the creative act is in Lobey's world. Spider points out that the other mathematician:

> was Goedel, a contemporary of Einstein, who was the first to bring back a mathematically precise statement about the vaster realm beyond the limits Einstein defined: In any closed *mathematical system*—you may read 'perceivable, measurable phenomena'—*which though contained in the original system, can not be deduced from it*— read 'proven with ordinary or extraordinary logic.' Which is to say, there are more things in heaven and Earth than are dreamed of in your philosophy, Horatio. There are an infinite number of true things in the world with no way of ascertaining their truth. Einstein defined the extent of the rational. Goedel stuck a pin into the irrational and fixed it to the wall of the universe so that it held still long enough for people to know it was there. And the world and humanity began to change. And from the other side of the universe, we were drawn slowly here. The visible effects of Einstein's theory leaped up on a convex curve, its production huge in the first century after its discovery, then leveling off. The production of Goedel's law crept up on a concave curve, microscopic at first, then leaping to equal the Einsteinian curve, cross it, outstrip it. At the point of intersection, humanity was able to reach the limits of the known universe. . . . (pp. 128–29)

It should be clear that the title of the novel is taken from this explanation. Spider's comments about the meaning and significance of Einstein and Goedel form the literary and philosophical center for what occurs in *The Einstein Intersection*. What we are to understand is that, as Spider tells Lobey, "There's just as much suspense today as there was when the first singer woke from his song to discover the worth of the concomitant sacrifice. You don't know Lobey. This all may be a false note, at best a passing dissonance in the harmonies of the great rock and the great roll" (p. 131). Spider is telling us, albeit indirectly, that the creative act today still has all the meaning and significance that it has always had. We are told that "Things passing in a world of difference have their surrealistic corollaries in the present. Green-eye creates, but what he creates is an oblique side effect of something else. You receive and conceive music; again only an oblique characteristic of who you are—" (p. 133). But though Lobey has understood much, he still fails to perceive the nature of his identity. He is, of course, a musician. This is clear from the first paragraph of the novel. Yet Lobey himself is unaware of what being a musician entails, that is, that he must continually commit himself to the creative act and all that that suggests. After all, Lobey has been told by Spider that "there are more things in heaven and Earth than are dreamed of in your philosophy, Horatio" (p. 128). It remains for Lobey to discover his nature and realize the full implications of what it means to be a creative artist. Once Lobey discovers himself, he will become a writer since he is a narrator agent who produces a noticeable effect on what he elects to present as his story.

The novel, then, grows out of two great systems of thought and justifies the idea that form is, after all, only an extension of content and nothing more. Yet it is equally clear that the theory Spider presents creates an implicit world view or, as I have preferred to call it, a physics. It is a physics because it explains the phenomena of Lobey's world and the way in which those phenomena take their shape and find their significance in relation to the narrator's own perceptual awareness of his world—its limitations and possibilities. It is also equally clear that whatever occurs in the novel is meant to be understood by making a comparison between the intersection of Einsteinian thought with that of Goedelian. The Goedelian triumphs since it reinforces the novel's literary dimensions. It does so because it admits the limitations of science while at the same time it gives "absolute" justification to man's art, his creativity. The concepts of mathematics and physics form the inner model to the novel as a fictional system. This system in turn forces us to realize that what a man can "truly know" is, in the final analysis, limited to the "prison house of his senses," to the familiar experiences of his world. Where physics and mathematics may suggest that there are limitations to man's abilities, they too, like fiction, release him into the far vaster realm of the imagination whose boundaries are determined and limited only by the creative act, by the power of the imagination. As Wallace Stevens has said, "We live in the mind."[15] Yet if we live in the mind, the things of the mind present themselves to us through structured systems, in this case, language, and the various forms which language may take are, in their own turn, the result of the imagination insofar as the imagination presents the possibilities of things.

What I want to suggest is that Delany's novel represents a shift in the art of the science-fiction novel and that this shift is understandable only in terms of the various premises that give rise to it. This shift in the art of the science-fiction novel is, to borrow an analogy from Judith Merril, "as though a figurative planet composed of man's intellect, suddenly acquired so much additional mass, or velocity (or both?) that it flew out of orbit, breaking up and fragmenting under the strain."[16] In other words, this shift in the art of the science-fiction novel is a result of a different way of looking at man and the world. The various premises which constitute this new way of looking at man and the world are of such a different order that they may be compared to the breaking up of a figurative planet and its assumption of a new orbit about the sun.

Ostensibly, the various themes of *The Einstein Intersection* are worked out in terms of myth, as I have already suggested. Delany informs us that "the central subject of the book is myth" (p. 78). Stephen Scobie in "Different Mazes: Mythology in Samuel R. Delany's *The Einstein Intersection*" suggests that " 'myth' . . . is not a simple or a unified concept."[17] Scobie identifies or discovers "(at least) three distinct *levels* of myth" in the novel (pp. 12–13). First, there is what he terms " 'fictional myth,' mainly Greek, the central references being to Orpheus, Theseus and the maze, and Pan. This is a mythology to which we do not give any *literal* belief, though we do admit that it carries a kind of 'truth,' in anthropological, social, or psychological terms" (p. 12). Second, Scobie notes that there is a " 'religious myth.' This is a mythology that is still alive as a religious faith: while few people today believe in Apollo, a great many do believe in Jesus Christ" (p. 12). And finally, there is " 'historical myth,' the main references being Billy the Kid, Jean Harlow, and Ringo Starr" (p. 13). Further, Scobie suggests that:

> Beyond these three levels of mythology, and such minor references to comic-book and movie serial mythology as "Spiderman" and the "cliffhanger" scene, there is one basic over-riding level. The characters of the book are not human; they are another race who have assumed the patterns of the human body and soul, and—as one of my students most concisely put it—they have made myths out of *us*. (p. 13)

Scobie is correct when he cites his student's remark that the characters of the novel "have made myths out of us." All of the character's names in the novel are suggestive of various fictional, historical, and religious figures. For instance, Lobey becomes Orpheus while at the same time his name suggests indirectly, perhaps, Lobo (wolf), though admittedly this connection is rather tenuous and is made only to suggest a certain character trait of Lobey's personality; that is, he is an individual alone in his world. Lobey's name, in the novel, is also linked to Ringo Starr and Billy the Kid. The Dove is, in the novel, linked to Helen of Troy and Jean Harlow. Green-eye becomes Christ or any great martyr and Spider "every traitor you've [Lobey] imagined" (Delany, p. 130). The purpose, of course, of using names as Delany has done in *The Einstein Intersection* is to deepen our sense of historical continuity in order to allow us to move into the future and see Lobey as a heroic figure. In a sense Lobey is a composite figure who exhibits the traits of great figures of the past while at the same time emerging as a unique figure. Although Scobie has understood much about *The Einstein Intersection,* in an important sense, he has missed the point of the novel, for he fails to perceive an other, more significant level to myth in the novel. If *The Einstein Intersection* treats the interface between Lobey and his memories (racial or whatever) and if it treats the interface between Lobey and his world, then it also treats the "human" problems which arise out of Lobey's relation to the phenomena and science of his world. What I am suggesting is that Scobie has overlooked two fundamental levels of myth in *The Einstein Intersection*. First, and most importantly, science itself becomes a myth in the novel. After all, Lobey has inherited man's science, or at least it would seem a safe assumption that he has inherited his science, since he tells us about it in his story. The actual science available to Lobey, however, may be less than that which was known to man, though the novel in several places suggests that the products of man's science—his "ships and projection forces . . . are still available to anyone who wants to use them" (Delany, p. 129). The presence of science in Lobey's world is comparable to what Scobie suggests about the function of fictional myth, that is, Lobey does not give any *literal* belief to what Spider tells him of the theories of Einstein and Goedel. Spider himself suggests:

> I want a Goedelian, not an Einsteinian answer. I don't want to know what's inside the myths, nor how they clang and set one another ringing, their glittering focuses, their limits and genesis. I want their shape, their texture, how they feel when you brush by them on a dark road, when you see them receding into the fog, their weight as they leap your shoulder from behind; I want to know how you take to the idea of carrying three when you already bear two. Who are you, Lobey? (Delany, p. 130)

Spider's interest in science is not functional; that is, he is not interested in putting science to work for him to achieve some type of control over the physical world, but rather he is interested in the shape and texture of science as an explanation for the existence of certain phenomena. Further, Spider's explanation of the meaning of Einstein and Goedel, though accurate, gives only the shape and texture of Einstein and Goedel's theories. I might also point out that Lobey's science *is* inherited in the same way in which the Greek myths of Orpheus, Theseus, and Pan and the myths of Billy the Kid, Ringo Starr, and Jean Harlow have been inherited. However, there is one important difference between science as a myth and the myths of the Greek Orpheus and the twentieth-century Billy the Kid. That difference is simply that Lobey's race is on the verge of rediscovering the power of science. In other words, science may exist as a myth in Lobey's world, but at the same time it holds out an explanation of the shape of his future, of the possibilities inherent in that future. Science, or rather the explanation of scientific thought which Spider presents to Lobey, forms the philosophical and conceptual center of the novel and suggests the possible solution to Lobey's understanding of the nature of the world and, since, as we have already seen, *The Einstein*

Intersection is concerned with the subject of myth, then science itself becomes a myth and serves a mythic function in the novel. *The Einstein Intersection* reconciles art with science (mathematical physics) and demonstrates that they are not incompatible interests or incommensurate ways of seeing the world. The reason for this reconciliation, once grasped, is quite simple. DeLong suggests that "just as indeterminateness, previously considered peculiar to imaginative creations, was found in the physical world with the discovery of the quantum theory, so indeterminateness was also found in mathematics with the discovery of the limitative theorems" (p. 59). The reconciliation between art and science which takes place in *The Einstein Intersection* is made possible by this understanding. This is clearly the case since the Einsteinian world of relativity places a premium on perceptual relativity while the world as Goedel conceived it emphasizes the indeterminate and irrational—both points of view which would have been impossible in classical physics. In a sense man's science has caught up with man's art. Nevertheless, the fact remains that the concepts of mathematical physics which stand at the center of the novel *explain* the nature of Lobey's world of physical (genetic and material) and psychic abnormality. The reconciliation which takes place in the novel between art and science and between classical and contemporary physics, of course, occurs ultimately in the creative act, in the imagination, and it does so since Lobey's story is an imaginative presentation of the possibilities of things. In other words, Lobey selects and "edits" his presentation from that which is implicit in his act of telling his own story. Lobey's act of telling his own story is implicit in the structure of the novel and its narrative technique and is one of the philosophical and creative consequences of the fact that what has been presented only points to what is implicit in what *was* presented.

The second level of myth in *The Einstein Intersection* which Scobie fails to identify is concerned with the nature of creation and the creative act. In *The Einstein Intersection* the creative act is given the status of a myth. Everything in the novel points toward this central fact—that the novel is a product of the imagination which presents, after its own fashion, a study of the creative process as it works itself out in Lobey's mind. The emphasis throughout the novel is on the *act* of doing or making something—music, and consequently, the novel. What Scobie fails to understand, then, are the implications of what is inherent in the conclusion he draws about the function of myth in *The Einstein Intersection:*

> The ending of *The Einstein Intersection* leaves everything still open to question. The individual response still has to be made: by Lobey, and by the reader. Mythology also is inconclusive: the pattern of the maze exists, but you must still create your own as you walk through it. Myths are not images, not answers. (p. 18)

Myths may not be "images" or "answers" but they do, as Geoffrey Hartman points out, "allow man to keep on functioning."[18] What Delany is saying, and has said several different times in *The Einstein Intersection,* is that the traditional myths (Greek or other) no longer serve the same function they once did. Myths live and die like fashions in the garment industry, though admittedly their life is longer. The creation of a personal mythology (Blake is a good example) is a response of the individual to the death of a more general pervasive mythology. This is why, in part, Spider wants "a Goedelian" and "not an Einsteinian answer" to his questions about mythology. This is why Lobey "may be Orpheus" or he "may be someone else" (Delany, p. 131). The reason, as Spider informs us, is that "The world is not the same. That's what I've been trying to tell you [Lobey]. It's different" (Delany, p. 131). Myths are models.[19] They establish a context which allows the individual a way of explaining the essentially mysterious and unfathomable nature of the world and life. They are pre-scientific explanations, if not prerational, and, as such, they "are productive of social cohesion."[20] Delany's response to the problem of mythology is to attempt to create a new mythology, one which emphasizes the creative nature of man and life and is not backward looking. This is why he leads us in *The Einstein Intersection* through the traditional myths of western society, from the past to the present. Billy the Kid, Jean Harlow, and the Beatles become, in *The Einstein Intersection,* the mythology of the twentieth century upon which Lobey builds his own *responses* to the indeterminateness of his world. If Lobey and his race "have made myths out of us," then we must conclude that the traditional myths (Greek, etc.) are wanting in some vital way. What they lack is, of course, functionality. Delany tells us, in an excerpt from his journal at the beginning to section twelve, that "Lobey starts the last leg of his journey. I cannot follow him there" (p. 136). The reason why Delany cannot follow Lobey in his journey is clear—the traditional myths (of Orpheus, Theseus, and Pan, or even of Ringo and Billy the Kid) are outworn and no longer serve their purpose. They are the responses of a *different* age and a *different* world to its own problems. What Scobie fails to understand is that artistically it is necessary first to present the old backward-looking myths in order to allow us to move through them and into a new response to the world. The creative act demands a new response, a new exploration. Delany may not be able to follow Lobey, since Lobey has fictional existence in his own right, but Delany, in his own way, does create his own response to the problem, and that response is *The Einstein Intersection.* Further, through the use of the quotations from the author's journal which are prefixed to the beginning of each section, Delany allows us to trace his own journey, its starting and stopping points.

The "historical" and "religious" myths of the novel, the ones Scobie identifies, are thematic and structural devices which are necessary in order to allow us to create a new and more powerful mythology, and that mythology is nothing less than science. Science, once seen and understood as this new mythology, is reflected in the very title of the novel. The intersection of the Einsteinian world of relativity with the Goedelian world of indeterminateness emphasizes the irrational and leads us only deeper "into a misty realm of symbolism and abstraction." Science cannot take us further than Goedel. Yet in that distance lies a remarkable achievement. For it suggests that a radical shift in the art of the science-fiction novel has taken place. It does so since the concepts of mathematical physics which Spider presents are used to "support" and justify the nature of the creative act. In other words, the metaphors (models) which form the framework and structure of the novel are scientific principles and concepts "with their ideal aim of corresponding to structures that 'really' exist in the universe forever unverifiable."[21] They are not drawn from nature but rather portray a relationship between various events and occurrences which take place in *The Einstein Instersection*. What I am suggesting is that our perception of a change in the art of the science-fiction novel and, specifically, in *The Einstein Intersection,* is dependent upon perceiving a shift in the way in which the narrator, in this case Lobey, sees his world. You cannot see or understand the novel through the lens of traditional criticism, for to do so is only to perceive, in the final analysis, the tradition.

The narrative strategy of the novel is dependent, then, upon Lobey's recognition that a shift has occurred in his visual-conceptual field. Lobey may be a futuristic Orpheus but, more importantly, he is a fictive "I" or eye, a consciousness made aware of the meaning of "difference" and its role in his world. Wayne C. Booth in *The Rhetoric of Fiction* points out that "as soon as we encounter an 'I,' " in fiction "we are conscious of an experiencing mind whose views of the experience will come between us and the event."[22] Lobey is a narrator-agent since he produces "a measurable effect on the direction of the events he selects to present as his story."[23] The fundamental problem of the novel demands a clear understanding of what is implicit in this type of narrative technique. That understanding involves the strategy which the narrator uses to tell his story. Obviously, Lobey is a musician. The novel begins significantly enough with a description of Lobey's flute-machete:

> There is a hollow, holey cylinder running from hilt to point in my machete. When I blow across the mouthpiece in the handle, I make music with my blade. When all the holes are covered, the sound is sad, as rough as rough can be and be called smooth.

When all the holes are open, the sound pipes about, bringing to the eye flakes of sun on water, crushed metal. There are twenty holes. (p. 5)

Lobey's flute-machete is significant in several ways. First, Lobey focuses our attention on his instrument as a physical device which serves a creative function—to make music. The emphasis in the opening paragraph is on the creative act—to make something happen, occur—and the possibilities inherent in that act. Yet Lobey, himself, is unaware at this point of the full meaning and significance of this act. The flute-machete may serve as a device for creativity, but it may also serve as a device for destruction—the musician's axe. Since our attention is initially focused on the object used in the creative act, it is clear that the user is an artist. What is more important, however, is our realization that this opening paragraph establishes the narrative point of view of the novel and informs us that Lobey will tell his own story. Though our attention may be initially focused on the story of Lobey who, like Orpheus, sets out on a journey (quest) to regain his lost love, the fact that the story has already taken place forces us to conclude that the author of his story, Lobey, has already discovered certain things about the nature of himself, his world, and his relation to that world. In other words, at least two stories exist in *The Einstein Intersection*. The first story, as told by Lobey, concerns an earlier history of himself as the artist (musician) who sets out on a journey to accomplish a specific end. As in all traditional quests, the protagonist will face certain hardships and trials. It is out of these "encounters" with the phenomena of his world that his experience will come into conflict with his understanding of that world. Likewise, the fact that Lobey is the narrator of his own story suggests that he has made certain discoveries about the nature of his world and his way of seeing in that world. These discoveries force Lobey to a new understanding of himself and his relation to his world. We never remember reality but only the memory of that reality, and our memory of that reality will, of necessity, be different from our actual experience of it. Lobey's problem, then, is an artistic one and demands that he make choices.

At the beginning of the sixth section of *The Einstein Intersection* Delany quotes John Ciardi's "How Does a Poem Mean" to the effect that "A Poem is a machine for making choices" (p. 65). The analogy Delany wishes us to make is clear. We should consider the novel a machine for making choices and the choices we make will be determined by our previous understanding of the creative process and its relation to the imagination. Though Delany's ploy is to call on authority, at this point in the development of the novel, to justify the idea of the possibilities inherent in the act of making a choice, it still remains for the novel to demonstrate

Lobey engaged in the act of making choices. And, after all, the choices Lobey will make are conditioned by the supposition that he has a purpose—to find Friza. Though Lobey may choose one route over another, the choice he does make will be directed toward what he understands as his goal. What he will discover, at some point in his journey, is that the basic nature of his goal has changed, and with his recognition of that change will come a different perception of himself and his world.

However, what is even more important than the fact that Lobey is a musician is the fact that he is an author. There is, then, the inner story of Lobey the musician who sets forth on a journey of discovery in his attempt to find Friza. In this respect the novel is quite traditional. Yet it is out of this quest that Lobey's confrontation with the phenomena of his world arises. The basic incongruities that arise out of this quest continually impinge upon his senses. Out of the familiar world the narrator has always known—the world of his senses—will grow the strange and unfamiliar, so that, in a sense, by the end of the novel, Lobey will have undergone a radical shift in his visual-conceptual field. He will see the world and himself with a difference. As Scobie notes, " 'Difference' and 'different' are the key words of the book; they recur on almost every page" (p. 14). Further Scobie correctly points out that not only is "the basic characteristic of their society [Lobey's] . . . change; its controlling myth is metamorphosis. Delany's major image for this is genetic mutation, but it is apparent also in the language and structure of the book" (p. 13). Consequently, the first paragraph of the novel serves several important functions. It establishes the narrative framework and point of view of the novel. Lobey is a reflective intellectual consciousness. It is interesting to note that the distance which separates Lobey as narrator from Lobey as musician is never great within the confines of the novel itself. He continually intrudes upon his story to remind us that he is telling it. The effect of this intrusion by Lobey into his narrative is to remind us that the story that is immediately in front of us is a device for taking us step by step to that point where we may realize that the real story is the one that emerges from Lobey's very act of telling his story. We may begin with relative stability in point of view, with relative harmony in Lobey's presentation of his world, but by the end of the novel this has all changed, and we are allowed to see an entirely different world from that with which we began.

Perhaps the most significant discovery Lobey makes is made in terms of his recognition that his world continually is engaged in change. Lobey informs us "the year I was born a rash of hermaphrodites" were born and "the doctors thought I might be one" (p. 6). Lobey's very birth suggests that it is indeterminate. Further, Lobey's quest for Friza becomes a journey towards discovery of self and the nature of identity. However, within the inner story of the novel Lobey, as musician, will never make this discovery. The discovery remains to be realized by the reader who comes to understand that Lobey, as author, is a narrator agent who has already arrived at the conclusion that his purpose and function is inseparable from the nature of his art. His function as author is to tell his own story; this is implicit in the narrative strategy of the novel and involves that which has been already discussed. Once Lobey discovers his identity, he does not talk about it but rather presents it—and that is *The Einstein Intersection*.

In *The World We Imagine,* Mark Schorer suggests:

> The virtue of the modern novelist—from James and Conrad down—is not only that he pays so much attention to his medium, but that, when he pays most, he discovers through it a new subject matter, and a greater one. Under the "immense artistic preoccupations" of James and Conrad and Joyce, the form of the novel changed, and with the technical change, analogous changes took place in substance, in point of view, in the whole conception of fiction. And the final lesson of the modern novel is that technique is not the secondary thing that it seemed to Wells, some external machination, a mechanical affair, but a deep and primary operation; not only that technique *contains* intellectual and moral implications, but that it *discovers* them.[24]

Under the artistic preoccupations of writers such as Samuel R. Delany, the narrative art of the science-fiction novel has changed. The final lesson of the novel may well be, as Schorer suggests, "that technique is not secondary . . . but a deep and primary operation." However, it has become increasingly clear that technique may not be separated from the subject matter it gives rise to and expresses in this novel.

The form of *The Einstein Intersection* grows out of this deep and primary operation concerned with the nature of technique. It is a technique which manifests a world view whose ideas come from the implications of Einstein's theory of relativity and Goedel's limitative theorems and which leads us to suggest that a new form of organicism has arisen. This "new organicism," however, unlike that of the nineteenth century, is not based on a set of metaphors which present us with a picture of nature. Rather, this "new organicism" finds its expression and justification in the abstract models science creates in its attempt to penetrate to the underlying structure of the universe. Further, these "scientific" models, rather than capturing the nature of reality, only present and define an event, thereby producing the radical shift in the art of the science-fiction novel which has been discussed here. Yet the very term "organic" itself seems limited in its ability to suggest what has taken place in the nature of the science-fiction novel since it seems to suggest that it is somehow in touch with nature. And, as I have shown, modern science (mathematical physics) never lays bare the underlying reality of the universe but only leads us forever deeper into the realm of abstraction and symbolism. But the symbols change. They may lead us deeper into abstraction, but the creative act remains the center to which all our efforts are ultimately directed. What we have seen, then, is that the creative act, like all products of the imagination, like science itself, is indeterminate. All we can possibly hope to accomplish is to illuminate the paths which the imagination takes in the hope that somehow knowledge will be the result, and that knowledge will be ephemeral and indeterminate.

What was presented in this chapter will be continued in the next; however, our attention will shift from *The Einstein Intersection* to Brian W. Aldiss's *Report on Probability A*. With this shift in scrutiny will come an exploration of a different set of aspects of the theory of relativity and the limitative theorems. For underlying both Einstein's and Goedel's theories stands a new way of looking at the universe (and the novel) in terms of statistical probabilities. Unlike *The Einstein Intersection*, however, *Report on Probability A* exhibits the principles of probability theory not in the overt fashion in which Spider presents the ideas of mathematical physics in *The Einstein Intersection*, but rather through the logical pattern of the parts of the novel and their relation to the whole.

3

Probability and the Principle of Uncertainty

> *Intelligibility still continues to be a basic assumption of the mind confronting the universe, and the capacity to predict future events still continues to be the primary criterion for the formulation of any natural law. But prediction is now limited to the probability, not the certainty, of future events. The whole definition of "intelligibility" has changed. It must provide for an area of uncertainty, hence of ambiguity, in our knowledge of the universe. At the same time, "structuring"—that is providing abstract models which bear coherent relation to the external world—continues to be the basic activity of the human mind. . . .*
>
> Sallie Sears, Georgianna W. Lord,
> *The Discontinuous Universe*

Given the theory of relativity and the philosophical implications of Kurt Goedel's limitative theorems and their significance within Delany's *The Einstein Intersection*, I argued that Lobey was inescapably a part of the world he wished to explore. Yet the very act of Lobey's exploration, and our realization of the fundamental significance of this act, forced us to conclude that if the novel was to fully realize the various premises that gave rise to it, both implicit and explicit, then these premises had to be worked out in terms of the form of the novel. In moving from Delany's *The Einstein Intersection* to Brian W. Aldiss's *Report on Probability A*, the object of our examination has changed but the ideas and concepts developed in the preceding chapter still remain, for behind the theory of relativity, behind Goedel and Heisenberg, stands modern probability theory. Because of this change in novels, it is now necessary to shift our focus within the field of modern mathematical physics, though the field itself remains unchanged. For *Report on Probability A*, like *The Einstein Intersection*, gives rise to a model which suggests a fundamental change has occurred in the expression of its form.

Form, as it was tentatively defined at the beginning of chapter 2, was conceived of as nothing more than an extension of certain basic ideas and concepts that were expressed in the novel; that is, I accepted for the moment Charles Olson's definition of form. I concluded, as a logical consequence of the implications of this definition, that the ideas and concepts that existed in *The Einstein Intersection* had resulted in a new organicism and that the very term "organic" seemed somehow to be lacking in its ability to describe adequately what had taken place in the art of the science-fiction novel. It is now necessary to modify our understanding of form if we are to understand the meaning and significance of probability theory in Aldiss's *Report on Probability A*.

Previous concepts of organicism have always presupposed a certain continuity of form; that is, organic form has been traditionally understood to consist of an unbroken and coherent whole greater than its parts. Yet one of the implications left unstated in the last chapter about organicism was that "organic form becomes discontinuous form" when understood in terms of the implications of the theories of mathematical physics and their significance in reshaping our understanding of the workings of nature.[1] Ihab Hassan in "Beyond a Theory of Literature: Intimations of Apocalypse?" argues that contemporary literature (not simply science fiction) is "characterized by 'unstructured and even random elements,' [and] undermines the idea of organic form on which formalist criticism in English is based."[2] I disagree with Hassan that contemporary literature is unstructured, though it may contain "random elements." Contemporary literature has structure but the nature of that structure is different from the structure of previous literature. I would agree, however, that the new structures that have arisen in the science-fiction novel undermine the idea of organic form. The reason for this undermining may be understood as the result of a shift which has occurred in the way in which science views nature. George Brecht in "Change-Imagery" suggests that "the conjuncture of statistical theory with mathematical physics, which occurred about 1860, resulted ultimately in a reformulation of our concept of the workings of nature; the requirements of strict causality, which classical philosophy had regarded as an a priori principle underlying the mechanics of the universe, were replaced by a measure of probability."[3] The "predominance of cause thus gave way to the predominance of chance," as consequence of this event, as Brecht points out, and "chance became an underlying principle of our world-view" (pp. 84, 86). Modern ideas about the nature of causality have been altered as a result of this event and must now include probabilistic prediction. It is only natural, then, to expect the novel to reflect these changes, although these changes may be felt only indirectly in their consequence for literature. And as Brecht points out:

> We only mean that the works of great artists are products of the same complex, interacting welter of cause and effect out of which came the results of mathematical physics. If we believe history to show that art of the past has fit into the cultural matrix of the time in which it was produced, we have incentive to look for the trends in contemporary art which are consistent with analogous trends in these other fields. (pp. 86–87)

The point to be made, however, is that the forms of the contemporary science-fiction novel have changed and these changes are the result of a change in the nature of our concepts about the workings of nature. The contemporary science-fiction novel has simply realized the significance of these changes and given expression to them in the form of the novel. In the place of the term "organic," consequently, I wish to substitute the word "wholistic." This substitution, I think, does not in itself change our understanding of the form of the novel but it does help us to overcome a tendency to think of the novel in terms of a set of metaphors which present a picture of nature rather than a model which presents a picture of our relation to nature. Further, by referring to the term "wholism" we remove ourselves, to some degree, from the implicit metaphor that the term "organic" always seems to suggest, that is, that a work of art is *like* a plant. What I am suggesting is that our understanding of the meaning of metaphor and what it represents has changed as a consequence of our changed understanding of nature. In previous literature metaphor has often presented an immediate comparison of one thing to another. Generally, the result of this comparison has been to create a picture of nature in the novel, and, therefore, a picture of the universe, often as a form of direct experience. The metaphoric expression of nature in the novel gave rise to a type of representation. Yet as science's view and understanding of nature changed, the ways in which that view could be expressed demanded that our understanding of metaphor change. Consequently, I argued in the preceding chapters that metaphor became a synonym for model. This distinction, it seems to me, is crucial and in keeping with the argument presented in chapter 1 and referred to above. Further, in chapter 2 I argued that the form of *The Einstein Intersection* was synonymous with a model that grew out of certain ideas and concepts which were implicit in the novel and that these ideas and concepts were taken from mathematical physics. I suggested that, in the final analysis, the model presented an event, an occurrence, and that at the "heart" of this event stood the creative act. I suggested that this act was indeterminate and that indeterminacy was characteristic not only of products of the imagination but that it was also characteristic of modern mathematics and physics. The idea of discontinuous form in a wholistic novel becomes central to what will be discussed in this chapter.

Brian W. Aldiss is England's most prolific and popular writer of science fiction (some 149-plus short stories and novels) and, of all his novels to date, *Report on Probability A* is, perhaps, his most experimental. It is experimental in the sense that it differs markedly from the accepted work of other science-fiction writers and departs from the mainstream of the contemporary novel, both American and English. *Report on Probability A*, like Delany's *The Einstein Intersection,* represents a fundamental shift in its form. The basic factor which seems to be responsible for this shift in the form of the novel is the central position which probability theory occupies in the novel, for the form of *Report on Probability A* grows out of the literary implications of probability theory used as a "structuring" device within the novel. In other words, probability theory provides the basis for an abstract model which gives rise to a literary realization of that model which is its form. Further, since the novel is limited in its possibilities to probabilities and not certainties, the form of the novel must take into account the indirect implications of the Principle of Uncertainty. It must do so since the Principle of Uncertainty is based on certain concepts whose existence is a consequence of what is inherent in the development of modern mathematical reasoning. Finally, in the movement of its style and technique, *Report on Probability A* is similar to the French *nouveau roman* and, specifically, bears more than a passing relationship to the novels of Alain Robbe-Grillet, since it demonstrates an affinity for many of the same concerns Robbe-Grillet discusses in *For a New Novel.*[4] Three sets of factors, then, seem to be responsible for *Report on Probability A*—the literary implications of probability theory in giving rise to an abstract model which structures the novel, the indirect implications of the Principle of Uncertainty, and the relation that apparently exists between the style of the novel and many of the problems of style discussed by Robbe-Grillet in *For A New Novel.*

Report on Probability A, like Delany's *The Einstein Intersection,* ends on the note that everything is expectation, that there are no certainties— only probable outcomes, probable courses of action, probable solutions— to the various possibilities presented in the novel. Further, as a result of the implications of probability theory, it is impossible to determine, with any certainty other than probabilistic, which interpretation of the novel is the "correct" interpretation or what events are the most significant events. As Robbe-Grillet suggests, "*possibilities* lurk in the corners—possible lives, possible literatures" and to this I would add, possible worlds (p. 130). The reason for these "possibilities" is that the very act of observation is involved in the fact that the novel seems to be a series of observations made in the form of a report. In other words, in its fictional dimensions the novel purports to be an impersonal observation (apparently a scientific report on an alternate universe labeled "Probability A"), though, in any final sense it is not, since the novel itself is the *Report on Probability A*. Another way of stating this is to suggest, as Robbe-Grillet points out, that:

> The book makes its own rules for itself, and for itself alone. Indeed the movement of its style must often lead to jeopardizing them, breaking them, even exploding them. Far from respecting certain immutable forms, each new book tends to constitute the laws of its functioning at the same time it produces their destruction. (p. 12)

Report on Probability A begins with the idea that alternative universes exist and, as one reviewer of the novel for *The London Times Literary Supplement* put it, these universes differ "from one another minutely or substantially; here [in the novel] they are 'in phase,' to the extent that they can observe one another by telepathic or mechanical means, according to their cultural pattern."[5] However, this same reviewer, who remains anonymous, tells us "Mr. Aldiss's novel is a commentary on an analogue of Holman Hunt's picture 'The Hireling Shepard [sic],' fixed eternally in its single ambiguous moment. What went before can be guessed at but never known; so also with what will come after." This reviewer is incorrect when he states that Holman Hunt's picture "The Hireling Shepherd" is "fixed eternally in its single ambiguous moment." The picture is only "fixed" if we assume that it is simply a picture which has "absolute" existence in any given universe, that is, if we assume that the picture may be observed only from a fixed point of observation from within a fixed system (universe) and that it has existence only in that system—an assumption which, in actual fact, is not warranted by the structure of the novel or the implications of the theories involved. The picture occurs in several different universes in the novel (since it is observed by various watchers in other universes and, therefore, also has "existence in those universes") and is given slightly different descriptions by Aldiss in each. There can be no doubt as to the picture's existence as a physical object in the different universes in which it appears, but it is not, in theory, the *same* picture. Each picture or rather each description of the picture shares certain basic elements or characteristics with the others—not only descriptively but in the various ways we may choose to interpret the contents of the picture and what those contents suggest. In other words, the different pictures which occur in *Report on Probability A* intersect at certain points and, therefore, share a common set of elements with each other. The question which logically arises, since each picture stands, in a limited sense, at the "heart" of each universe it occurs in, is whether or not the universes in which the picture occurs constitute reality or whether the picture is itself reality, or a mirror image of that reality, or whether it is simply a device which ultimately allows "seeing" between the various universes, or whether it serves some other function. To complicate matters, the picture is presented at the end of the novel outside of any of the universes described in the novel. This raises the question that if the picture presented at the end of the novel lies outside of the universes presented in the novel then in what universe does it occur? The answer is deceptively simple and constitutes the "essence" of the novel; that is, the universe which it occurs in is *Report on Probability A*—the novel. Further, since the novel constitutes a probabilistic working out of the possibilities of things, it is clear that its existence occurs in our universe, as a result of our observation and, therefore, in the imagination. It should also be pointed out that the appearance of "The Hireling Shepherd" suggests a symbolic function in terms of the various universes in which it appears. In a sense, "The Hireling Shepherd" represents or suggests that it is the *subjective* correlative to the universes it appears in while at the same time suggesting that the universes themselves, rather than being objective, are in fact subjective. Yet it is equally clear that since the picture lies outside any of the universes presented descriptively within the novel, it, in turn, presents its own subjectivity; that is, it constitutes the laws of its functioning while at the same time tending to destroy those laws. Consequently, at the end of the novel, not only are we presented with a "description" of the novel but we are also presented with a realization of the contents of the picture which only suggest a probabilistic solution to how we are to interpret that which was presented in the first place. Further, there is the very "real" danger that the reader (like the *Times* reviewer) will mistakenly assume that the picture exists at the *heart* of an inner world the novel creates. The reader may assume for various reasons that the novel creates an inner world, a *heart* so to speak, that exists. In actual fact, however, all is surface in *Report on Probability A* and no attempt may be made to penetrate to an underlying reality which may or may not exist, for the novel has no *depth* in the traditionally understood sense of that word. What is being suggested is that the reader initially may assume that something is contained in the novel and therefore perceive the existence of an interior world when in fact none exists. The reasons for this are two-fold. First, the nature of the universes presented, when understood in terms of probability theory and modern cosmology, are simply surfaces and, second, the concept of "metaphor" plays a limited and special role in the novel. Robbe-Grillet points out that for him "the *surface* of things has ceased to be . . . the mask of their heart, a sentiment that led to every kind of metaphysical transcendence" (p. 24). The significance of this lies in part in understanding Robbe-Grillet's proposition about the nature of metaphor. For Robbe-Grillet, "Metaphor . . . is never an innocent figure of speech" (p. 53). He explains:

> To say that the weather is "capricious" or the mountain "majestic," to speak of the "heart" of the forest, of a 'pitiless' sun, of a village "huddled" in the valley, is, to a certain degree, to furnish clues as to the things themselves: shape, size, situation, etc. But the choice of an analogical vocabulary, however simple, already does something more than account for purely physical data, and what this *more* is can scarcely be ascribed only to the credit of belles-lettres. The height of the mountain assumes willy-nilly, a moral value; the heat of the sun becomes the result of an intention. . . . In almost the whole of our contemporary literature, these anthropomorphic analogies are repeated too insistently, too coherently not to reveal an entire metaphysical system. (p. 53)

The point which Robbe-Grillet makes is that "metaphor, which is supposed to express only a comparison, without any particular motive, actually introduces a subterranean communication, a movement of sympathy (or of antipathy) which is its true *raison d'être*" (p. 54). Consequently, Robbe-Grillet's novels are marked by an absence of metaphor, though as he is quick to point out, his statement[s] "in no way constitute a theory of the novel" but "merely attempts to clarify several lines of development which seem to . . . [him] crucial in contemporary literature" (p. 9). Aldiss's novel, on the other hand, is not as characterized by the absence of metaphor, though the metaphors which do occur in his narrative are, initially, to be perceived as "objective." By this I mean that the metaphors occur in a specific context which, because the novel is a report, suggest that they be understood as "objective" rather than introducing, as Robbe-Grillet points out, a "subterranean communication" (p. 18). In spite of this, however, they do not achieve "total impersonality of observation," though Robbe-Grillet would argue that "*freedom* of observation should be possible, and yet it is not" (p. 18). The reasons for this lack of "objectivity" in what constitutes a *report* is in part the fault of a misconception of what a report may be. Further, the use of metaphor in Aldiss's novel is in part a function of how we understand the idea of probability in the novel and its relation to the theory of relativity. In the previous chapter I pointed out that, according to modern mathematical physics, we must take into account the *fact* of our observation; that is, the observer and the observed are not separated but rather joined in the *act* of observation. Metaphor does occur in *Report on Probability A* and gives in its immediate context the appearance of objectivity, though in terms of its relation to the novel as a whole, it is not objective. However, I should make the distinction here between the metaphors contained in the narrative and the metaphors which give rise to the novel. In a novel such as Walter Tevis's *The Man Who Fell To Earth,* the structural form of the novel is contained in or rather framed by reference to Brueghel's painting "The Fall of Icarus."[6] This analogy or metaphor is suggested by the title of Tevis's novel and is supported throughout by the actions of its protagonist. Consequently, when I speak of the metaphors which give rise to the novel I am not referring to those "limited" metaphors which occur in any given sentence in the novel but rather I am referring to the larger principles which define and pattern (structure) the novel. Yet these metaphors, as I suggested in the previous chapter, are not so much metaphors in the traditional sense as they are models which constitute the laws of the novel's "functioning at the same time that . . . [these laws] produce(s) their destruction" (Robbe-Grillet, p. 12). And, as J. Bronowski in *The Common Sense of Science* explains:

> The model sets up behind the machine [*Report on Probability A,* in this case] a hypothetical world which yields the same ends. . . . That is, the model defines a set of fundamental units, and states that, if the real world were in fact made up from these units, obeying these laws, then its behaviour would coincide with what we observe.[7]

Aldiss's *Report on Probability A,* unlike Delany's *The Einstein Intersection,* does not, then, set up an inner model which, after its own fashion, gives rise to the novel. Rather, in a sense, as Bronowski suggests in "The Discovery of Form," "The pieces have lost (or almost lost) their own meaning, and the structural or logical pattern is in complete command."[8] There does not exist in the novel an inner world created by the novel which serves as the conceptual counterpart to the novel understood as a whole. It is the overall movement of the novel which constitutes in its various parts the laws of its functioning. These parts which make up the novel and, therefore, make up and give rise to the model, are based on a literary realization of what is inherent in probability theory. The model is mathematical (abstract) in nature and is created from an understanding of the implications of elementary probability theory. For instance, it is possible to *describe* the novel, in a limited mathematical way, in terms of probability theory. A. M. Arthurs suggests in *Probability Theory* that "in general, if there is a rule by which we identify abstract concepts with physical objects, then, we have what is called a *mathematical model* of the real process, and different models can describe the same empirical situation."[9] Obviously, we are not dealing with physical objects in *Report on Probability A*, except in the limited sense that the novel describes its own physical world, a world that will contain physical objects which are real in terms of its own system of definition and creation. In fact, the novel contains a great amount of description (initially understood as "objective") of physical objects—clocks, houses, paintings, newspapers, pigeons, etc., and the various spatial-temporal relations they bear to each other.[10] For instance, in "Part One" we are told:

> A single window on the north-west side of the house reflected the light back in a dull fashion, without movement, except once when the reflection of a pigeon, wheeling above the garden, splashed across it. No movement came from the house. No sound came from the house. . . . G lived not in the house but in a wooden bungalow in the garden, overlooked by the window set high in the northwest side of the house. The bungalow, which contained only one room, measured about five by four metres, being longer than it was deep. It was raised above the ground on low pillars of brick. (pp. 7–8)

The bulk of the novel consists of this type of descriptive delineation of the *relative* position of the various characters presented in the novel with relation to the physical objects that exist in their world. Things, objects, are given. They exist and, as Robbe-Grillet points out, "if I say, 'The world is man,' I shall always gain absolution: while if I say, 'Things are things, and man is only man,' I am immediately charged with a crime against humanity" (p. 52). Further, Robbe-Grillet declares that:

> The crime is the assertion that there exists something in the world which is not man, which makes no sign to him, which has nothing in common with him. The crime, above all, according to this view, is to remark this separation, this distance, without attempting to effect the slightest sublimation of it. (p. 52)

The novel as a *report* attempts to "remark this separation," to show, in the final analysis, that there is no recourse but to realize that there exists something in the world which is not man and that this something has nothing in common with him. However, Arthurs points out that:

> Any mathematical model involves idealization, and our first idealization concerns the possible outcomes of an "experiment" or "observation." If we want to construct an abstract model, we must decide what constitutes a possible outcome of the (idealized) experiment. To illustrate this, consider the "experiment" of tossing two coins. How do we list the possible outcomes of this experiment? It may be done in a number of ways, depending on what we are interested in. For example, we may be interested in whether each coin falls heads (H) or tails (T). Then the possible outcomes are (H,H) (H,T) (T,H) (T,T)? Every outcome of the experiment corresponds to exactly one member of the set. (pp. 9–10)

By "set" Arthurs is referring to the fact that "in all probabilistic reasoning there is a basic framework consisting of a set called the sample space, and subsets called simple events, which have probabilities assigned to them" (p. v). A set "is a collection of objects thought of as a whole. The objects, of which the set is a collection, are called elements or members of the set" (p. 1). In *Report on Probability A* the *sample space* is represented by the novel itself and the *elements* of S (the *sample space*) by the various parts of the novel, that is, by "Part One—G Who Waits," "Part Two—S The Watchful," and by "Part Three—The House and the Watchers." Subsets, that is, sets contained within larger sets, may be represented by the various sections of each *element* of the *sample space*. For example, the various *elements* (represented by "Part One," "Part Two," and "Part Three") may contain subsets represented by, in the example of "Part One," the sections numbered consecutively 1, 2, 3, . . . 6 and so forth for the other *elements*. In Arthurs' example given above concerning the possible outcome of whether a coin falls heads (H) or tails (T) we might be interested instead "only in whether the coins fall alike (A) or different (D). Then we could list the possible outcomes as (A)(D), giving, on allocating probabilities, a second model of the experiment" (p. 10). In the case of *Report on Probability A* even an idealized model of the various outcomes possible becomes quite sophisticated and complex and, depending upon the type of operations we perform, many different models may become possible. Obviously, such an attempt as the above description in which we have tried to describe the novel using the notation of probability theory reveals, however, little or nothing about the *literary* realization of probability theory in the novel. As a literary realization of probability theory, *Report on Probability A* is a working out of the probabilities inherent in its structure and made known to us by the various ideas and concepts presented in the story in terms of its form. In other words, Aldiss demonstrates in the novel that "reality" itself is but a reflection of a probabilistic way of looking at the universe and that the novel is a literary realization of what is implicit in probability theory. That which appears to be the real world turns out, after all, only to be a probable world with no way of ascertaining the reliability of one model, or interpretation of that model, or of another.

Briefly, according to the *London Times* reviewer, the novel presents a meticulous description of "a single small corner of the world similar to, though not identical with our own."[11] And, as this reviewer points out, this world

> is being scrutinized, in italics, by a blurred railway junction of a character called Domoladossa, while a recession of further universes, also italicized, scrutinize him.

> In the world of the report, too, scrutiny bulks large. The scene is the garden of a shadowy, possibly jealous, recluse named Mr. Mary; the scrutineers, living in squalor in three separate out-houses on scraps brought to them surreptitiously by Violet, the daily, are the ex-gardener G, the ex-secretary S and the ex-chauffeur C; what they scrutinize, chiefly, is the enigmatic, possibly beautiful Mrs. Mary. G visits the cafe opposite Mr. Mary's house run by a Mr. G. F. Watt (sic, presumably intentionally). . . . A pigeon—'designated X' is stalked and at last killed, by a cat not designated anything in particular. Towards the end Mr. Mary brings his wife something in a glass, she pushes it aside, and he slaps her. On this flurry of activity the ambiguous moment switches off, leaving us fruitlessly examining the marginal symbolism—road accidents, funerals, bicycles, bicycle tyres, a mandala—for clues to what is suppose [sic] to have been going forward.[12]

What the novel suggests, or rather what we may infer from this state of affairs, is that perhaps Mrs. Mary has had affairs with each of her observers. Yet there seems to be nothing in the novel of the tangible sort of evidence which would allow us to make this type of statement with any certainty at all. Further, in the novel, all is suggestibility and inference; beyond this we cannot go, though it should be possible to engage in a type of speculation or conjecture about the possible meanings and outcomes of what is presented.

Prefixed to the beginning of the novel is a short but significant quotation from Goethe:

> Do not, I beg, you, look for anything behind phenomena. They are themselves their own lesson.

This quotation has significance in several important ways. First, it introduces us to phenomenological psychology and, second, it provides the psychological justification for the inability of the various observers in their different universes to penetrate with their science into the "human universe" of the world they are scrutinizing. The fundamental principle of phenomenology, according to Maurice Merleau-Ponty in his essay "What is Phenomenology?" is that "perception is not a science of the world, it is . . . not an act, a deliberate taking up of a position; it is the background from which all acts stand out, and is presupposed by them."[13] Further, phenomenology rests on the proposition of the complete and unique autonomy of the individual's perception of reality. Phenomenology attempts, as Merleau-Ponty suggests:

> to give a direct description of our experience as it is, without taking account of its psychological origin and the causal explanations which the scientist, the historian, or the sociologist may be able to provide. (p. 357)

In *Report on Probability A* Domoladossa purports to be a scientist who is engaged in the act of observing, in the three parts of the novel, the worlds of G, S, and C. In actual fact he is engaged in reading a report apparently prepared by someone else for him, perhaps by his subaltern Midlakemela. The point to be made, however, is that Domoladossa is a scientist who is limited in what he sees by what he reads. His knowledge of the alternative universe he observes is indirect and, as Kuhn suggests, "The scientist can have no recourse above or beyond what he sees with his eyes and instruments."[14] There is a limit to what instrumentation, regardless of its refinement, can reveal. For one thing it cannot tell us much about a man's thoughts, his emotions and motivations, except insofar as we may infer what those emotions and motivations may be from his actions. Domoladossa is limited by conjecture to the world he observes in the same way in which we are. One of the stratagems of the novel, then, is to allow us, like all the observers, the privilege of observing the existence of physical objects and events yet not allowing us to see beneath the surface. This stratagem also holds for what takes place within the world of the report. Goethe's statement, then, provides us with a direct sort of account of the way in which we are to understand the various phenomena presented in the novel. As the scientist can have no recourse beyond what is presented to him by his eyes and instruments, so too, the report limits what may be seen and understood. Another way of looking at this situation in the novel is by understanding that its internal processes suggest an analogy between what science may reveal and what literary art may be concerned with. In one sense, the novel demonstrates the limitations of science while at the same time showing that literary art is also limited. If science can tell us nothing about the nature of the "human" universe and cannot penetrate it, likewise literary art can tell us nothing about the nature of the physical universe. This may seem like a contradiction. It is not. All that is being suggested is that initially, the assumptions we make about the nature of how we perceive something to exist must, of necessity, begin from a point of view which is at best ambiguous. Phenomena may be in themselves their own lesson, but we should not confuse the *existence* of phenomena with the way in which we perceive those phenomena to *have* existence. Goethe's statement, then, serves an important function since it provides a "clue" to how we must understand that which is presented in *Report on Probability A*.

In "Part One—G Who Waits" we are told:

The Report begins:
   One afternoon early in a certain January, the weather showed a lack of character. There was no frost or wind; the trees in the garden did not stir. There was no rain,

although anybody accustomed to predicting rain might have forecast it with a fair expectation of being right before nightfall. Clouds lay thickly over the sky. The face of the sun was not visible. Consequently, shadows had no form. (p. 7)

What is interesting about this opening is the fact that we are told that what we are about to read (and have read) is a *report*. However, a report need not be scientific (objective) in the sense that, for example, an article in *Scientific American* may present the results of a study concerned with some physical phenomena. A report may consist of a highly subjective evaluation about the nature of the state of existence of something. In other words, the reader may initially fall into the trap of making a set of unwarranted assumptions about that which he is about to read. Yet in the final analysis, as we move through the novel, we come to understand that that which was read was a report and that it does initially presuppose a limited type of objectivism. Nevertheless, what is presented in the above passage is a rather subjective evaluation about the immediate state of certain phenomena as they exist in the physical world. The "suggestive indefiniteness" of the passage—"in a certain January," and the fact that the evaluation establishes the idea that "anybody accustomed to predicting rain might have forecast it"—suggests that what has been presented has been "colored" by a perceiving consciousness. In other words, the narrative point of view is omniscient, as it is throughout the novel, with respect to the report itself. Yet this omniscient voice is prejudiced in what it reports since instead of presenting simply a description of the setting, it biases its description by drawing conclusions about the way in which the "weather," "wind," "sun," and "shadows" have existence. Another way, perhaps, of stating this idea is to suggest that since what has been read purports to be a report, then, the report presumes the existence of a reporter and the existence of the reporter in turn presupposes a certain position of observation, from which the report has been made. This position of observation, after its own fashion, demands that we understand that, after all, what was presented is subjective and has effaced, to some degree, the distance that exists between the reporter and the things reported. Toward the end of the first section of "Part One" the report is interrupted by an italicized passage which reads, in part, as follows:

Domoladossa looked up from the long report.
"Mr. Mary's wife," he said. "We think she may be the key to the whole matter. I shall be interested to see what the report makes of her."
"The main object of the report is directed towards a different objective," Midlakemela said. "Let us call this continuum we are studying—the one containing Mr. Mary and his wife—Probability A. We know it is closely related to our continuum, which I like to think of as Certainty X. Nevertheless, even superficially, Probability A

reveals certain basic values that differ widely from our own. It is our first duty to examine those values." (p. 14)

With the beginning of this passage we learn for the first time that what we have been reading is a report as seen through the eyes of someone else—Domoladossa—and that alternative universes exist. Further, it is clear that the title of the novel comes from this passage. The world of "Probability A," that is, the world inhabited by G in "Part One," and later in the other parts of the novel by S and C is a probabilistic world which will, because of its very nature, differ in several important ways from that of "Certainty X"—the position of observation from which Domoladossa and his colleagues are involved in studying the alternate universe. The "objective" of the report is not to study Mr. Mary's wife but rather the "basic values" that exist in "Probability A" and the ways in which those values differ from the values which exist in Domoladossa's continuum. What is important about this passage is the idea that as Domoladossa is engaged in the act of studying a report about "Probability A" from the position of "Certainty X," we too are engaged in observing the universe of the novel from our own position or continuum. Domoladossa's continuum acts as an analogical counterpart to our own process of studying the novel. And, as basic values differ between Domoladossa's universe and that of "Probability A's," likewise, there will exist differences between our values and those observed in the novel. Further, an important point to make here is that what we observe to exist in the novel will be limited not only by the relative position of our observation but also by the limitations imposed upon us by the methods we use to carry out our scrutiny. For instance, Domoladossa informs us that "Probability A's time-flow rate seems to differ from our own. . . . Instrumentation is being devised so that we can have the absolute scales by which to measure such discrepancies" (p. 15). Yet all observation, in theory, is relative to the limitations that exist within the system from which that observation is being made. Instrumentation (technology) fundamentally interferes with the relation of man to nature and vice versa. As Heisenberg points out:

> The claim of science to be capable of reaching out into the whole cosmos with a method that always separates and clarifies individual phenomena, and thus goes forward from relationship to relationship, is mirrored in technology which step by step penetrates new realms, transforms our environment before our eyes, and impresses our image upon it.[15]

It is impossible, then, to establish an absolute scale or position of observation without violating the current theories of mathematical physics. What is being suggested is that Domoladossa's position of observation is not "fixed" in any absolute sense but is dependent upon the relationship that exists between his own continuum and that which he is engaged in studying. One of the consequences of this relationship is that the report Domoladossa is reading is itself an interpretation and, since it is an interpretation, it immediately calls into question not only the validity and reliability of what has been reported but also the very process of the observations made which resulted in the report. The report (in roman), then, before it is interrupted by this first italicized passage, has simply presented an almost "static" description of a character named G who, as we learned, was an ex-gardener who worked, at some point in his past, for Mr. Mary. Section 1 consists of a description, somewhat factually given, of G's world and its relation to Mr. Mary (and others) and Mr. Mary's house. The location of G in his world (universe) is made relative to the existence of Mr. Mary's house. This type of locating of people and objects and things within the report is paralleled within Domoladossa's universe by the same assumption; that is, "Probability A" may only be observed from the position of "Certainty X." The position of the observer is initially assumed to be fixed and to have existence relative to the thing observed. Further, what is being suggested by analogy is that the observer (watcher) can only define his position of observation relative to that which he is actually involved in observing. Later in the novel what we will discover is that the statement that man confronts only himself is valid in the age of relativity. Sometimes later in "Part One" we learn from Domoladossa that "the report is all very meticulous, but there's much it leaves out" and Midlakemela informs us that "we can take nothing for granted. The laws of our universe may not obtain there" (p. 25). Both watchers, Domoladossa and Midlakemela, are apparently aware to some degree, at this point in their examination of the report, of the limitations that their universe—"Certainty X"—imposes upon the nature of their observations of "Probability A." Domoladossa informs us that this is "quite" the case but that "what interests . . . [him] is that the psychological make-ups of these people, G, Mary, and the rest may be alien to us. They may LOOK human, but they may not BE human" (p. 25). The point is, of course, that there exists no way by which Domoladossa's study may reveal anything about the "psychological make-ups" of these "people" they are studying. In section 5 of "Part One" we learn that:

> As he read, Domoladossa felt a sense of privilege. A week ago, he and all his millions of fellow men were living in a world of apparent uni-probability. Then this other continuum manifested itself. Who knew, there could be a myriad [of] different probability worlds? But he was one of the first to read the report on Probability A.
> He experienced danger as he read. This house, and the outhouse S was entering—they were so banal that you'd never look at them twice in ordinary life. But did

Probability A contain ordinary life? Or would the fact of their all being the same make the whole business even more miraculous?

And this was just Probability A. A myriad of probabilities. . . . The Gods had been not merely prodigal but mad.

A photograph of his wife stood on Domoladossa's desk. He gazed at it tenderly. There would be continua where they had never met, of course. . . . Then he returned to the report. (pp. 37-38)

In this passage as well as in the other italicized sections of the novel, we have, in a sense, been allowed to penetrate into the minds of Domoladossa and Midlakemela. The point of view is omniscient and this omniscience provides us with the privilege of observing Domoladossa's thoughts and feelings. Yet it should be clear that this passage suggests that what appears as an omniscient point of view is not that at all but rather it suggests that there may exist other universes, other continua, each with its own set of observers observing Domoladossa, Midlakemela, "Certainty X," and "Probability A," and that this passage is in fact part of another report, a report being scrutinized by some yet unidentified group of watchers. And, perhaps, the reader of the novel is the ultimate "watcher." Further, it should be noted that as Domoladossa studies his report on "Probability A" his attention is focused on a photograph of his wife. In section 5 of "Part One" we are told that:

Domoladossa pencilled a note in the margin of the report: "She [Mrs. Mary] was singing."

He wanted to add, "She was happy," but that would be carrying the job of interpretation too far.

He was almost breathless with the thought of the happiness of his alien woman, a happiness that the impartiality of the report seemed to heighten. He considered the passage he had just read extremely erotic, and wondered how the Governor would take to it.

Eagerly, he read on. (p. 47)

The analogy Aldiss wishes us to make between Domoladossa and ourselves is clear. Like Domoladossa, we should not carry the "job of interpretation too far," that is, we should limit ourselves to the facts as they are "impartially" presented rather than engage in conjecture or speculation about what these facts may seem to mean, for we have no way of ascertaining what they mean. In other words, the things of the report are just that—things, objects, and they exist separate from man. Yet man himself, that is Mr. and Mrs. Mary, G, S, and C, are themselves objects in the novel—surfaces, which we can never penetrate except by conjecture. In the final section of "Part One" we are privileged once again to look into Domoladossa's mind and examine it. We are told by our "omniscient" narrator that Domoladossa conjectures, "Suppose this strange world, this Probability A, was so strange it knew no sin? Suppose God had a myriad of worlds, all lying there like nursery beds, in which He tried out various combinations of sin or innocence?" (p. 22). The crucial word in this passage, as it is throughout the novel, is "suppose," for "suppose" is simply another way of stating a conditional supposition; that is, what we learn is based on a supposition and, therefore, involves probabilities and not certainties. It is also in this last italicized passage of section 6 that we learn that Domoladossa and his world—Certainty X— are being observed by someone else:

> As he conjectured, Domoladossa's eyes rested on the desk photograph of his wife. From beyond its convenient frame, the Distinguishers were watching him.
> There were four Distinguishers on duty at present, all standing gravely in the open air, gazing at the tall manifestation, on which Domoladossa could be seen at his desk, leafing through the report.
> "He looks much as we do."
> "Obviously, a world of almost co-determinate synchronicity."
> "But we have no key to scale."
> "Scale?"
> "He may be no bigger than my thumb. He may be as tall as a house."
> "Keep watching. His entire probability-sphere may evaporate at any minute, like a puff of steam." (pp. 55–56)

It is clear, then, that the analogical process established in the novel between watchers being watched by watchers becomes an increasingly sophisticated one. As Domoladossa is engaged in studying a report of "Probability A," from the position of "Certainty X," so too, "Certainty X" is being scrutinized from the position of the Distinguishers, who exist in a world of almost "co-determinate synchronicity." However, there remains another dimension to "Part One" that we have yet to comment on and that is the world of "Probability A"—the world Domoladossa scrutinizes. We too, like Domoladossa, must read the report (which we have) and what we discover, of course, in the report is the same process of observation at work. We learn a basic amount of factual detail such as, "Approximately two years had passed since G began living in the wooden bungalow" and that Mr. Mary had built it as a "summer house" for Mrs. Mary (pp. 8–9). We are told that "The wooden bungalow had been constructed facing the north-west side of the house. It did not face it squarely, but at an angle of some twenty degrees, in the direction of east-southeast" and that the "objects" which existed inside the bungalow "were few in number" and had been brought over by his wife, "before they had quarrelled" (pp. 9–10). Most of "Part One," then, consists of either a description of physical objects and the spatial-temporal relations they bear to each other or of a description of G's process of observing Mr. and Mrs. Mary, S, and C, though S and C do not figure prominently in "Part One." There exists a great deal of description devoted to objects "connected directly or in a more tenuous degree with the passage of time" and to mirrors or looking-glasses (pp. 10, 12). Indeed, it is these latter objects, mirrors and glasses, which emphasize the entire process of observation within G's world and which are important, for they provide us with a means, initially, for understanding what is involved in the report at large. For instance, early in "Part One" we are informed that "a mirror or looking-glass was fixed to the window frame at such an angle that, as G sat on the wheelback chair, he could look at the mirror and see reflected in it a part of the garden not otherwise visible from where he sat" (pp. 12–13). This process of observation, suggested by the various descriptions of physical objects used in "seeing," introduces the idea of perceptual relativity and suggests that what is important is the very process of observation and not the thing observed since to observe the existence of something reveals only that it has existence, a surface, and that it is impossible, in any final sense, to penetrate beyond the surface of that which is presented to begin with. We are forced simply to accept the existence of the phenomena, though we may question the nature of their existence. Later in "Part One" when our attention shifts to S, this process is made clearer by the introduction of a passage which describes a telescope S had bought before Mr. Mary had dismissed him. We are told that "On the barrel of the smallest tube, the legend 22X was engraved, signifying that the telescope was capable of magnifying objects glimpsed through it twenty-two times" (p. 40). Further, we learn that S

> was now viewing the world through five thicknesses of glass, four consisting of the lenses in his telescope and one of the small square panels of glass that formed the centre of the nine glass segments together comprising the round window. These layers of glass lent their slight coloration to the view. (p. 41)

In this passage we learn, as we have seen elsewhere, that our perception is "colored" not only by our "instrumentation" but by our "thoughts"; that we can never see the world *clearly*. There exist only degrees of "clarity" and these degrees of "clarity" are dependent on the nature of our involvement in what we are observing. Obviously, telescopes do not present us with the greatest degree of magnification. In a novel, for instance, such as Michael Crichton's *The Andromeda Strain*, we are told that "increasing vision is increasingly expensive" and the novel supports this claim by tracing the increasingly sophisticated and expensive use of various types of "optical" instruments.[16] In *The Andromeda Strain* we move from the world of our eyes outward from a pair of binoculars to reflector and refractor telescopes, to radio astronomy while at the same time we move in the opposite direction, that is, to optical microscopes, electron microscopes, and finally to X-ray crystallography. The movement is from the relatively large to the relatively small, from the relatively small to the relatively large, from microcosm to macrocosm and from macrocosm to microcosm. Yet, the continual refinement of our technological apparatus, though it may reveal the existence of new and unknown worlds, still does not allow us to penetrate beyond the surface of the existence of things. The point is that there exist limits to the world of "sight" and those limits are not all inherent in our technology but exist within ourselves. Consequently, in *Report on Probability A,* the emphasis on scrutiny, on observation and "seeing," only stresses the inherent limitations and possibilities of that process. We can know nothing beyond what our eyes and instruments present us with. Within *Report on Probability A,* within the report, within the world of G, there exists a picture. This picture we have already in part discussed in an earlier section of this chapter. However, this picture, that is, the picture of "The Hireling Shepherd," serves the same function for G as does Domoladossa's photograph of his wife. It *awakens* the observers, in a sense, to the possibilities and, therefore, to the probabilities, of their worlds. At the beginning of section 2 in "Part One" we are told that "G was looking at a black and white reproduction of a painting hanging slightly above and to the right of a cupboard of unpainted wood. The reproduction was mounted and framed in a frame of varnished wood" (p. 18). Further we learn that:

> The subject of the picture was a rural scene. Sheep grazed, hay stood in stooks, wheat ripened. In the foreground, a country lad, possibly a shepherd, wooed a girl. The girl looked at the country lad doubtfully. Flowers grew, apples lay by the girl's skirt. (p. 18)

The relative "impartiality" of this description of "The Hireling Shepherd" is deceptive, for it is highly suggestive. What this picture suggests, like all of the universes and worlds described in the novel, is uncertain and indeterminate. Structurally, the function of the picture in the novel is to move us in the opposite direction from that in which we have already moved; that is, to move us from an outward process of observation of the report as seen through Domoladossa's eyes, to the Distinguishers, and so forth, in the other direction. We move from Domoladossa's report and scrutiny of Probability A (G's world) into that world, and from that world we move into the world presented by the picture, so that by the end of the novel the invented world which the picture presents becomes its world and reality. Further, by analogy, as the picture has a frame which contains something—a picture—so too, all of the worlds and universes (continua) described and presented in the novel are framed and that frame is, of course, nothing less than the narrative technique of the novel. That is, the novel's frame is its point of view. The novel is framed by a point of view which is omniscient, yet that very omniscience is conditioned only on our recognition of it; that is, the "impartiality" of the report assumes stylistically an omniscient point of view without the existence of an omniscient narrator. In other words, the omniscient point of view of the report and the novel is only a convention. The final point of view which controls and structures the novel is first person; that is, we can see the novel only through our own eyes. And, our own "seeing" will be biased and limited in the same way in which all of the characters' observations in the novel are biased and limited. This, then, is the lesson of the novel—that "phenomena" are "themselves their own lesson." Like G, Domoladossa, and others, we too are trapped by the very nature of our universe. We can observe the existence of these other worlds only by recognizing the inherent limitations of our own. I pointed out in chapter 1 that the theory of relativity was based on a philosophic analysis which insists "that there is not a fact and an observer, but a joining of the two in an observation" and it is this very joining, of myself with the novel and its characters, that proves not only the relativistic nature of the novel in terms of its structure but the realization that we, like G, are prisoners of the world of sight. In the report we are told that G's attention moves from the picture of "The Hireling Shepherd" to the rain which has started to fall outside of his "house":

> As G sat looking at the picture, his mouth came slowly open. His gaze became unfocused.
> Still the rain persisted. It ran slantingly down the panes; when G got up from where he was sitting in his wheelback chair and gazed through the panes, they made a knotted visibility of the corner of the house that was available to his eyes. (p. 19)

Quickly following this passage we learn that "for a short while, as the room darkened into obscurity, it seemed by comparison that the two windows grew brighter and glowed with their own light; then they faded to become two patches in the dark, and the man [G] was left to be in his own universe" (p. 20). The point to be made here is that our sense of sight can take us only so far before we are thrust back into our own world with its limitations and possibilities; before we, too, are left in our universe.

Structurally, it should be clear that in "Part One" the "contents" of the report, Domoladossa's world, and that of the Distinguishers is of little or no significance. What is of significance are the various relations which exist between Domoladossa and the report, between Domoladossa and the Distinguishers, and so forth, through as many combinations as are possible to list within the framework of the novel. Each report and each set of observers in themselves lack importance. They are important only because they present themselves as a process in which observation becomes the key to understanding the structural relationship of one universe

Probability and Uncertainty 65

to another. Yet, obviously, as we have been told, there are differences between the various alternate universes and these differences introduce the idea of uncertainty and indeterminancy; that is, we may speculate or conjecture about the meaning and significance of what we observe but we will never know with absolute knowledge that our conjectures are accurate or reliable.

"Part Two" which presents "S THE WATCHFULL" opens with an italicized passage which moves us clearly into the world of the Distinguishers and with this shift in our point of observation will come a different set of facts. We are told in the novel that "The Distinguishers stood on their hillside, solemnly staring at the curious mirage in the air, on which was a representation of a world to which they had only just discovered limited access" (p. 57). Further, we also learn that:

> The screen depicted a man called Domoladossa, who was leaning comfortably back in a chair, doing nothing but reading a report. Domoladossa was as occupied by his report as the Distinguishers were with him. The affairs of his life were forgotten while he followed the activities of an unknown man called S, who saw fit to examine the back door of a house through his telescope. (p. 57)

These passages allow us to continue to see the report on "Probability A" which Domoladossa was involved in scrutinizing. However, we now see the report from the point of view of the Distinguishers, through their eyes, which in turn present Domoladossa's viewpoint which presents the report. In other words, with the appearance of each new set of watchers and universes the type of information we receive is further restricted in certain ways, yet out of these restrictions also come other possibilities. Put a slightly different way, each new set of watchers adds another set of lenses to those we must look through in order to see "Probability A." Further, the greater the distance becomes between these universes, the less similar they will be. For instance, immediately following the above passage we find ourselves back in the report on "Probability A." But is it the same report as that which we saw through Domoladossa's eyes or is it some other report? The answer is uncertain and indeterminate. S, like G, however, has a picture by W. H. Hunt called "The Hireling Shepherd," which is fixed by a nail to a "cross-beam just above S's head" as he sits in the garage observing G, C, and the Marys. We learn from the report that the painting was as follows:

> Reproduced in black and white, the picture bore a legend in the white margin below it which read: "W. H. HUNT: The Hireling Shepherd (Oil, 1851)." Two figures were depicted in a sunlit rural scene. The left-hand figure was the hireling shepherd whose flock of sheep waited in the background. The hireling shepherd had caught a death's head moth and appeared to be displaying this insect to the second figure, a girl who

> sat with a lamb upon her lap. The hireling shepherd leant close against her to demonstrate his capture; since the girl with the lamb on her lap appeared to have removed one of her outer garments, the nature of their past, present, and future relationships was ambiguous. The girl looked over her right shoulder with an expression that also was ambiguous. Her mouth appeared pale, with an ample lower lip that perhaps pouted slightly; her eyelids drooped as she looked askance at the man. On some occasions it seemed to S that she regarded the hireling shepherd with a sort of indolent contempt, on other occasions that her expression was one of lazy complaisance. (p. 62)

There are several things of importance and interest in this description of "The Hireling Shepherd." First, it is much longer than its original description in "Part One." Second, the implicit ambiguity of the picture is for the first time mentioned, that is, that the picture is subject to more than one interpretation. Third, the description of the picture is expanded to present a fuller background of objects and our attention is now directed to include the presence of the "death's head moth." Overtly, the principle involved in the inclusion of various descriptions of this picture in the novel is structural. What is happening is that as we become further and further removed from the original report the novel began with—the report of Domoladossa's on "Probability A"—the more the universe that constitutes the picture will be expanded and vice versa. After all, we have been told that the picture presents an "invented scene" and that this invented scene is ambiguous—it defies our attempts to penetrate it and determine the meaning and significance of what it purports to present. The analogy we should make here is transparently simple: that as the picture is an invention, so too is the novel. In section 2 of "Part Two" the picture reappears once again. We are told that "Slowly his [S's] gaze began to move over the room. It fastened on a picture framed and hung on the cross-beam nearest to him" (p. 66). Further, we learn that:

> The picture was a representation in black and white of a man and woman in a rural setting. In the background might be seen a flock of sheep and a cornfield bathed in sun, the two divided by a grassy land shaded by willows growing on either side of it. In the foreground, on a bank covered with flowers, were two people, depicted at a moment which left their motives forever in some ambiguity. One of these figures was of a country girl. On her knee rested a lamb and two apples; two more apples lay beside her. It could be presumed that the girl was feeding or attempting to feed the lamb with the apples. (pp. 67–68)

Each time the picture appears in the narrative something new is added to its description so that what is happening is a gradual process of disclosure about the nature of the contents of the picture. And each time this description occurs it allows us to make another type of speculation or conjecture about the significance and meaning of what is presented. The point about the picture is, as we quickly learn, that "if there was anything behind this phenomena [the picture], if it was not its own lesson, then, it could be interpreted to mean that although the girl in part leant away from or was averse to, the advances of the shepherd, there was nevertheless, a part of her that inclined towards him, or was predisposed to accept his advances" (p. 68). Further, we are told:

> This ambiguity [the picture's ambiguity] . . . could hardly be resolved by a scrupulous examiner, since the rest of the picture seemed to echo rather than resolve the ambiguity. (In the same way, the scrupulous examiner was unable to decide permanently whether the creator of the picture had marshalled his objects with a deliberate attempt at a discomforting ambiguity or obliquity of statement, or whether he had aimed at making some form of statement incapable of paraphrase and perhaps not previously attempted, and in so aiming had not entirely succeeded, lapsing instead into an ambiguity that was unwished for.) (pp. 68-69)

Obviously this passage, in a sense, describes the same problem the novel presents, that is, we may recognize the principles at work and their significance but we will never be able to resolve intellectually or conceptually the meaning and significance of the various characters and their motivations in the novel. Any solution we do formulate to the problems of the novel will be probabilistic in nature and, therefore, involve a degree of uncertainty. Following this statement about the ambiguity of the picture, the report (whichever one it may be) is interrupted once again by an italicized passage which returns us not to the world of the Distinguishers but to Domoladossa's continuum. Domoladossa declares:

> 'Really, . . . this is too bad! Here is this long and increasingly pedantic description of a mediocre painting hanging in the coach house. What's more it has already been described once, and that was quite enough. Such an item must be quite irrelevant to our main interest.' (p. 70)

Domoladossa's attitude toward "The Hireling Shepherd" is quite understandable in terms of the information he has supplied us with earlier in the novel, that is, that "Probability A reveals certain basic values that differ widely from our own. It is our first duty to examine those values" (p. 15). Yet Midlakemela raises the question that the picture may not be as "irrelevant" to their study as Domoladossa seems to think. He questions, "Do you think so?" and Domoladossa replies, "I do think so! Don't you?" (p. 70). Midlakemela excuses himself from Domoladossa's presence and "reports" to Domoladossa's superior—the Governor. Midlakemela comments that "there is one curious item [in the report] which has just come up" (p. 70). "Well?" the Governor asks, and Midlakemela replies briefly that:

> It's a picture, sir, hanging in the loft above the coach house where S is hiding. From its description, it might well be the same picture that G has hanging in his wooden bungalow, which the report describes only briefly and in general terms. We're getting

68   *Probability and Uncertainty*

> a much more ample report of it now. It seems to be a bit fishy that the same picture should hang in both places. (p. 70)

Midlakemela's "intuition" that the occurrence of the picture in more than one universe seems to him "a bit fishy" is an indication of its significance and suggests that as the report progresses the painting will become increasingly important. Soon after, the Governor asks Midlakemela if they (Midlakemela) "Could . . . check on it." (p. 70). A quick check is made in an encyclopedia and it is determined that "the painter exists in our [the Governor's] probability-world, just as in Probability A" (p. 71). Following this request of the Governor's, the italicized section breaks off and we return to the report and to a continuation of the discussion of the painting. What follows in the next two pages (roughly) is a theoretical discussion of the possibility that the painter (W. H. Hunt) could have "created a second representation of this same imaginary scene, setting it fifteen minutes . . . ahead of the existing representation" (p. 71). We immediately learn that:

> Many doubts could then have been resolved, for one paradox of the existing picture was that its ambiguities were engendered by the fact that it showed only one moment on its time scale. Suppose that the second representation, depicting the same scene some fifteen minutes later, could be produced. It too would only show one moment on its time scale; but by comparison with the earlier moment in the first and existing picture, it would make much clear. (pp. 71-72)

The same type of "supposition" might be made for the entire novel, that is, suppose that each part of the novel depicts the same scene sometime later. These reproductions (representations?), then, would make much clear in terms of each preceding reproduction. In a limited sense, of course, this is just what has been happening. Yet, after all, this constitutes only a supposition and the supposition may not be proved with certainty. What we learn is that "the imaginary picture remained imaginary [as does the novel], and the existing picture remained open to torturing interpretation" (p. 72). The report continues for two paragraphs and is once again interrupted (broken) by an italicized passage which takes us back into Domoladossa's world (continuum). However, we quickly move in this passage from Domoladossa to the Distinguishers who are engaged, significantly enough, in observing Domoladossa "through the photograph of Domoladossa's wife on his desk" (p. 73). Photographs and pictures, in other words, become in the novel devices for "seeing" into other universes while at the same time they remain either reproductions of "reality" or imaginary inventions (creations). In either or both cases, their function within the novel suggests   analogy based on our own examination (interpretation) of the novel; that is, the novel is either a fictional system (an imaginary invention or creation) or a reproduction of reality and, therefore, in either or both cases becomes a device for allowing us to perceive the existence of another universe. And, of course, that other universe is *Report on Probability A*. Yet the nagging suspicion exists that if this other universe is *Report on Probability A,* then what universe do I exist in? In other words, the internal processes and analogies which exist in the novel have their analogical counterpart in our own examination of the novel and force us to conclude that the novel has no existence outside our own consciousness of it. This conclusion forces us to a further conclusion that we ourselves are a part of the novel. It is not possible to create a completely logically consistent system, fictional or otherwise, without presupposing the existence of a point of observation (place or system) external to the original system from which our observations are being made. In phenomenological terms what I am suggesting is that the novel is "dead" and exists (non-phenomenologically), according to Maurice Natanson in *Literature, Philosophy, And The Social Sciences,* in a "kind of catatonic suspension" waiting "for the mind of the reader."[17] What is happening, then, in the novel with its various descriptions of events and characters is that a series of analogies is established which allow us, like the various watchers in their own continua, to observe what is taking place in still other universes. The photograph which the Distinguishers look *through* and into Domoladossa's universe is paralleled by the existence of the novel which, for ourselves, serves the same function. The invented and imaginary become inseparable from the real and are no longer distinguishable as separate things. Toward the end of this italicized section—the one in which the Distinguishers observe Domoladossa through a photograph—we move one step further away from the original report which Domoladossa scrutinizes since we are introduced to a "robot fly" which follows the Distinguishers as they leave the hill on which the "image" of Domoladossa and his universe have "materialized":

> As they [the Distinguishers] walked down the hill, a small robot fly followed them. As vision was transmitted to a vast receiving set in a second-storey hall in New York, a group of men, several of them in uniform, stood or sat watching the transmission.
> At a raised dais, a technician under orders from the statesmen present was controlling the flight of the robot fly.
> Congressman Sadlier turned to his companion.
> "You see, Joe, that's the way it is. We've broken though at last—though what or where we've broken through remains to be seen."
> "A plurality of worlds . . . ," Joe muttered. As a radio communications engineer, he felt he should come up with some bright suggestions; but at the moment only vague poetic associations filtered through his head.
> Unaware of his multiple watchers, Domoladossa was showing the Governor the next part of the report. (pp. 73–74)

Sometime later in section 4 of "Part Two" we learn from Congressman Sadlier that "All we are after is facts. We don't have to decide what reality is, thank God!" (p. 96). The process of the novel is clear, the worlds of G, S, and C are opened by Domoladossa's report, which in turn is rapidly superseded by the Distinguishers, who in turn give way to Congressman Sadlier, who is followed by an even vaguer group which seems to be preoccupied by religious questions concerning the interpretation of "The Hireling Shepherd." The members of this group consist of a Suppressor of the Archives, ten jurymen, the Wandering Virgin, the Impersonator of Sorrow, The Image Motivator, and others. With the appearance of each new universe and group of watchers the worlds which they represent become increasingly dissimilar to the world of "Probability A" as the distance from "Probability A" is increased. That is, the farther removed an observer's world is from "Probability A," the less his world will resemble "Probability A." "Part Two" ends with an italicized section which returns us to Domoladossa, the Governor, and Midlakemela. We are told by the Governor that "We know there's an ex-gardener camping out more or less permanently in the summerhouse, and an ex-secretary camping out in the old stable. Now we're given to understand there's an ex-chauffer hiding out over the garage! Quite unbelievable! (p. 107).

At the beginning of "Part Three" we return to Congressman Sadlier and his universe, but this gives way to another group in section 4 which contains the President and an organization called "CKS" (p. 144). This group, however, is only known to the Suppressor and the Wandering Virgin and apparently not to the others (pp. 144–45). Further, "Part Three" contains another group composed of a father and his son who "stood in an empty warehouse staring at the manifestation [of Domoladossa] in puzzlement" (p. 124). The little boy asks his father "What is it Daddy?" and to this question the father replies, "We've discovered a time machine or something."

> He leaned farther forward; it was just possible to make out Domoladossa reading his report, for the New York screen showed the hillside manifestation revealing him at his desk. (p. 124).

Throughout the report which Domoladossa has been scrutinizing, the same type of description occurs for S and C which I have discussed earlier in terms of G. Further, we have learned from Domoladossa at the end of section 1 in "Part Three," that he has come to the conclusion that the alternate world he has been studying involves nothing less than a "human problem" (p. 118). His recognition of this is significant since he has come to understand that his science, his observation of "Probability A," will reveal nothing beyond the existence of that world and its objects. He cannot penetrate, as can none of the characters in the novel, the human universe. In the penultimate italicized section to the novel we are told that:

> Domoladossa went home to his wife that evening in a preoccupied fashion. He was trying to puzzle out, incidentally, how the events were interfered with by reason of their being observed. (p. 153)

Domoladossa's recognition of the fact that his observation of the events that have taken place in "Probability A" has interfered with those events is, of course, nothing more than Heisenberg's Principle of Uncertainty as it is given literary expression in the novel. The italicized passage continues:

> Others, too, felt the sense of mystery. Corless sat alone on the hillside, guarding the manifestation, in hourly anxiety in case it went away as suddenly as it had come. Joe Growleth packed up before the usual late afternoon rush to New Jersey began, but throughout an evening spent with his two wives, Peggy so charmingly white, Sophie so charmingly black, he remained preoccupied. The two men took the little boy home but phoned the police and then wondered if they had done the right thing.
>
> And there were watchers watching them, and they too had watchers, who also had watchers, and so on, and so on, in an almost infinite series. Every stage of watcher had a theory about the watched; every stage put something of its own passions into the watching.
>
> Sitting quiet in her own room, the fingertips of one hand resting in her tawny hair, Mr. Mary's wife sat at her own screen and regarded the cycle of universes as night closed in. (pp. 153–54)

The novel—*Report on Probability A*—is a closed or open (depending on your point of view) universe which opens itself up to the possibilities of things, but these possibilities are worked out in terms of probability theory and its implications in terms of the form of the novel, for the form of the novel is broken and interrupted by each appearance of a different universe and its watchers. And, of course, the final watcher is the reader of the novel *Report on Probability A*.

Imagistically, the novel ends as it began with the suggestion of rain and its prediction, or possibility of prediction: "Rainclouds drew over the sky, darkening it still further, until the peaked outline of an old nearby coach house was lost" (p. 156). The final lines of the novel are italicized and read as follows:

> Forgetting his flock, the youth leant forward, so that her sturdy form touched his chest and arms. As she half-turned, her hair was against his cheek. He could smell the warmth of the scents of her body, which the sunny day released.
>
> Nobody was near. The sheep could take care of themselves. Within his imprisoning hand, he could feel the doomed moth flutter. Her hand was raised toward it in a gesture of indecision.
>
> She waited.
>
> He waited. (pp. 156–57)

Report on Probability A began with what seemed to be nothing more than a report on "Probability A." Yet, as the novel progressed we discovered that what seemed to constitute "reality," that is, "Probability A," gave way increasingly to a description of "The Hireling Shepherd," so much so that by the end of the novel we have moved from a description of "The Hireling Shepherd" into the picture itself and the world it presents. The novel, consequently, ending as it does, leaves us "hanging" in the ambiguous expectancy of another world and universe— that of the youth and girl who are waiting, waiting like all the characters in the novel for the occurrence of something; and that something is nothing less than a resolution to the problem of deciding what all the various events which have been presented in the novel mean. What is their significance? To this question there can be no answer. For the question is meaningless as we have seen. What is significant is the very process of observation and that process is intimately bound up with the overall logical structure and pattern of the novel which grows out of the principles implicit in the assumption of alternative universes and their relation to one another. In other words, the logical structure and pattern of the novel is in complete command and the parts have lost all significance in and of themselves. The italicized passages represent, as well as do the non-italicized parts, sides of the same coin. In attempting to interpret the novel I have simply echoed it, by following the various principles implicit in the novel and the way in which these principles are worked out with respect to its overall form. For clearly, the form of *Report on Probability A* is discontinuous, since the very nature of the universes presented within the novel presuppose a certain openness. That is, since observation has taken place in thenovel between one or more universes, then the nature of those various universes must be relativistic and discontinuous at some point or points. Those points of discontinuity are a function of the nature of observation and rest on probabilities and not certainties, on the implications of probability theory given literary expression in the novel. Further, the narrative strategy of the novel is omniscient, but its omniscience is a guise or appearance which is false. It is an implied stratagem of report writing to give the appearance of "objectivity" when, in fact, none exists. Omniscient narration in the traditional novel always presupposes absolute knowledge of the events and characters it purports to present. However, in *Report on Probability A* our omniscient narrator is nothing more than an observer (watcher) who presents what he observes. He does not control the events he observes but is involved with them. And, as Heisenberg would suggest, is "no longer in the position of an observer of nature [the events and universes of the novel], but recognizes . . . [himself] as part of the interplay between man and nature" (p. 134).

4

Time and the Structure of Reality

Much of the obscurity that has surrounded the Theory of Relativity stems from man's reluctance to recognize that sense of time, like sense of color, is a form of perception. Just as there is no such thing as color without an eye to discern it, so an instant or an hour or a day is nothing without an event to mark it. And just as space is simply a possible order of material objects, so time is simply a possible order of events.

Lincoln Barnett, *The Universe of Dr. Einstein*

Slaughterhouse-Five, Kurt Vonnegut, Jr.'s anti-war novel, departs radically from the traditional chronological narrative of the nineteenth century and from almost all other science-fiction novels written during the first half of this century. This departure is unusual since, as Brian W. Aldiss points out in his history of science fiction *Billion Year Spree,* "The twentieth century was, for well over half its length, to prove but the nineteenth in extension, sharing magnified versions of its problems and triumphs. And its science fiction."[1] Further, Gary K. Wolfe in "The Limits of Science Fiction" suggests that "experiments with narrative time sequence are practically unheard of in science fiction, and yet the problems involved with time as an isolated concept are a staple of science-fiction writers from Wells to Asimov."[2] Wells's *The Time Machine* (1895), as its title suggests, was based on the idea of time-travel in which a narrator was aided in his explorations of the past and future by a machine. Yet this novel, and dozens of others like it which were to follow, was nothing more than a novel of remembrances in which the narrator looked back in time through the aid of his memory and presented, after a chronological fashion, the events he had witnessed in his travels in time. The absence of experiments with narrative time sequence in science fiction and, especially, in the science-fiction novel, perhaps may be explained by applying Ockham's razor—that the best explanation is the simplest and involves the least number of unknowns.[3] The explanation is simple enough and involves nothing more than suggesting that most science-fiction writers have shown little concern for their craft. Most science fiction, as Wolfe would agree, is "dismally incompetent in terms of even the most elementary fictional techniques" (p. 32). Perhaps the major reason for this "incompetency" resides in the way in which the writer saw and understood the possibilities of science fiction, since he saw science fiction, for the most part, as restricted or limited to simply a literature of ideas in which craft played a minimal role. Writers such as Verne and Wells may have had as their subject a truly different, if not new, set of ideas, but they expressed these ideas in an already existing and ready-made form—that of the nineteenth-century novel. For writer after writer, throughout the first part of this century, simply "pours" his story into an already existing mold as he discusses and plays with the implications of modern science. The typical science-fiction novel constitutes nothing more than a chronological (historical) presentation of a set of events which issue from some problem (usually extraordinary) that may be resolved only by the application of a scientific idea or principle. Typical of this state of affairs, of this kind of novel, is Fred Hoyle's *The Black Cloud,* in which the appearance of an "intelligent" cloud from outside our solar system unwittingly threatens the existence of man by its presence in our sky. The novel traces, through the eyes of a narrator who has lived through them, the events from the discovery of the cloud and its appearance in our sky to its departure from our solar system. *The Black Cloud* is a traditional novel in which Hoyle discusses the implications of twentieth-century science in dealing with the cloud and how those implications (and those represented by the presence of the cloud) may affect man. Written in 1957, *The Black Cloud* exhibits the form and structure of most twentieth-century science-fiction novels though in its form and structure it remains a nineteenth-century novel. Science fiction, then, for the most part, has not emphasized experimentation with the narrative time sequence of the novel. The writer's concern for his craft has seriously lagged behind his treatment of various ideas which grow out of scientific principles and concepts.

In the traditional novel of memory, including most science-fiction novels, the narrator simply begins at the beginning and traces the sequence of events, incidents, or anecdotes as they chronologically occur. This sequential presentation of events, more often than not, presupposes a historical or linear concept of time. In his essay "Chronology, Character and the Human Condition: A Reappraisal of the Modern Novel," M. A. Goldberg suggests that "the full title of Charles Dickens's novel—*The*

Personal History, Adventures, Experience and Observations of David Copperfield," points "with clarity to . . . [the] assumption, that the human personality and the varied adventures it undergoes between birth and death are best understood through chronological arrangements."5 In Dickens's novel we begin at the beginning (the first chapter is titled "I am Born") and follow the protagonist's adventures as he reports them chronologically to their end. However, this is not the case with Kurt Vonnegut, Jr.'s *Slaughterhouse-Five*. The difference, in part, between nineteenth-century novels like those of Dickens and *Slaughterhouse-Five* is a result of a shift in world view which is felt in the contemporary science-fiction novel, however indirectly, in terms of the narrative technique of the novel. This shift rarely is accounted for in the contemporary science-fiction novel but, rather, is assumed since the world "pictured" in that novel is different from the world pictured in the nineteenth-century novels. Fundamentally, the difference, in brief, is between Newton's conception of the universe and that of Einstein.

In a Newtonian universe time is conceived of as an absolute having existence (duration) independent from any system of reference. Its most likely form of expression in literary art is through the metaphor of a river. As Martin Gardner notes in "Can Time Go Backward" (*Scientific American*, January 1967), "this representation of time as a river has no older 'image.' "6 For instance, as Gardner points out, "In James Joyce's *Finnegan's Wake* the great symbol of time is the river Liffey flowing through Dublin, its 'hither-and-thithering waters' reaching the final lines, then returning to 'river-run,' the book's first word, to begin again the endless cycle of change" (p. 98). However, in the theory of relativity time does not exist as an absolute. According to Lincoln Barnett, "Einstein discarded the concept of absolute time—of a steady, unvarying, inexorable universal time flow, streaming from the infinite past to the infinite future."7 "For Relativity tells us," as Barnett observes, "there is no such thing as 'now,' independent of the system to which it is referred" (p. 48). Further, Barnett suggests that "The subjectivity of time is best explained in Einstein's own words" (p. 47). Barnett quotes Einstein to the effect that:

> The experiences of an individual . . . appear to us arranged in a series of events; in this series the single events which we remember appear to be ordered according to the criterion of "earlier" and "later." There exists, therefore, for the individual, an I-time, or subjective time. This is in itself not measurable. I can, indeed, associate numbers with the events, in such a way that a greater number is associated with the later event than with an earlier one. This association I can define by means of a clock by comparing the order of the given series of events. We understand by a clock something which provides a series of events which can be counted. (p. 47)

Barnett further points out that "by referring our own experiences to a clock (or calendar) we made time an objective concept. Yet the time intervals provided by a clock or calendar are by no means absolute quantities imposed on the entire universe by divine edict" (p. 47).

As A. A. Mendilow tells us in *Time and the Novel,* "Time affects every aspect of fiction: the theme, the form, and the medium—language," and he points out that "everyone in fiction as in life carries his own time-system about with him in a sense wider than that intended by Einstein when he coined the dictum [the theory of relativity]" (p. 31).[8] Another way of stating this concept is to suggest that time does not exist independent of the system to which it is referred. *Slaughterhouse-Five* and, to a somewhat lesser degree, *Report on Probability A* for example, are based on a relativistic conception of time. The structure of *Slaughterhouse-Five* is not based on clock or calendar time. Rather, the novel's structure is based on the theory of relativity and its implications. Time, in *Slaughterhouse-Five,* structures the events as they are presented through the memory of the narrator. The underlying structure of the novel is based on a nonlinear conception of time. Robbe-Grillet in *For a New Novel* suggests that "in the modern narrative, time seems to be cut off from its temporality. . . . Here space destroys time, and time sabotages space. Description makes no headway, contradicts itself, turns in circles. Moment denies continuity."[9] The structure of *Slaughterhouse-Five* is clearly discontinuous (broken) and wholistic inasmuch as the memory (both past and future) of the narrator is discontinuous. As memory is a psychological faculty which structures the presentation of its events, it will of necessity also present a conception of time which is the intimate function of the world that those events recall. In other words, the principles of relativity are inherent in the very way in which the narrator sees his universe and creates his story.

In "Chapter One," as well as elsewhere in the novel, we are given a great deal of what seems to be autobiographical information about Kurt Vonnegut, Jr. by the fictive "I" of the first paragraph. The narrator of the novel tells us that:

> All this happened, more or less. The war parts, anyway, are pretty much true. One guy I knew really *was* shot in Dresden for taking a teapot that wasn't his. Another guy I knew really *did* threaten to have his personal enemies killed by hired gunmen after the war. And so on. I've changed all the names.[10]

Without exception criticism of the novel has identified this "I" with Vonnegut himself. For instance, Tony Tanner suggests in "The Uncertain

Messenger: A Study of the Novels of Kurt Vonnegut, Jr.," "Since Vonnegut himself enters his own novel from time to time (like Hitchcock in his films) it becomes difficult to hold the various fictional planes in perspective."[11] It may be difficult to hold the various "fictional planes in perspective" but to assume that Vonnegut enters the novel from time to time is to confuse the author of the novel with his creation and to commit a critical error in understanding the novel. The error committed is the biographical fallacy. Obviously the novel contains autobiographical elements drawn from the author's personal life but to confuse these elements with the fictive "I" of this opening chapter is to misunderstand the novel and how time functions in it. The point to be made is that *Slaughterhouse-Five* is a fictional system; it is a novel and not a thinly-disguised autobiography. Further, the fictive "I" of this first paragraph of the novel is, in theory, not the author of the novel but rather a character who incidentally bears the same name. In other words, the problem this opening presents raises a question about the plausibility or credibility of not only the narrator of the novel but also of the nature of the novel itself. The problem is similar to that which is presented by Hemingway in *The Green Hills of Africa* since this novel contains a character named Hemingway, who also bears more than a passing resemblance to the author of the novel. Wayne C. Booth in *The Rhetoric of Fiction* points out that:

> It is a curious fact that we have no terms either for this created "second self" or for our relationship with him. None of our terms for various aspects of the narrator is quite accurate. "Persona," "mask," and "narrator" are sometimes used, but they more commonly refer to the speaker in the work who is after all only one of the elements created by the implied author and who may be separated from him by large ironies. "Narrator" is usually taken to mean the "I" of a work, but the "I" is seldom if ever identical with the implied image of the artist.[12]

The distance which separates the implied author of the novel—the novelist's "second self" or "public image"—from that of his inner expression of that self—the "I" of the above paragraph—has been, for all practical purposes, effaced. Yet we must accept this "I" as a fictional character who sets out to tell us his own story in terms of a modern day allegory. In one sense, the strategy of the novel is to present us with a novel about writing novels. This is clearly the case since we are told by this "I" that "I would hate to tell you what this lousy little book cost me in money and anxiety and time" and this, of course, is nothing more than a ruse or strategem for this "I" to do just that—tell us what *Slaughterhouse-Five* did "cost . . . [him] in money and anxiety and time" (p. 2). Consequently, since we must accept the "I" of this opening paragraph as a fictional character and not as the author of the novel, then, it is possible to interpret in a different light the meaning and significance of "All this happened, more or less." What is being suggested is that this "I" is to some degree, like his own creation—Billy Pilgrim—schizophrenic. This would explain why the narrator (the fictive "I") questions at the outset of the novel the veracity of the story (fictional or otherwise) he is about to present and is actively engaged in the act of presenting. The narrator's schizophrenia allows him to question which parts of the novel did happen and which parts did not, which parts are "true" and which parts are imaginary or invented. From another point of view this narrator is simply questioning the nature of "reality," what constitutes reality and distinguishes it from products of the imagination.

It would be appropriate here to recall Robbe-Grillet's remark that "moment denies continuity," for *Slaughterhouse-Five* is composed of a series of moments presented out of the narrator's perception of his world, its nature, and his understanding of the "inner" story he creates about Billy Pilgrim. The spatial and temporal connections which marked the chronological narrative of the nineteenth-century novel have, in *Slaughterhouse-Five,* given way to an entirely different understanding of time which displaces the Newtonian conception of time as an absolute. Time, in *Slaughterhouse-Five,* becomes relativistic and personal. Lincoln Barnett points out that "In our minds we tend to separate these dimensions [the three dimensions of space and the one of time]: we have an awareness of space and an awareness of time. But the separation is purely subjective; and . . . space and time separately are relative quantities which vary with individual observers" (p. 70). Further, Barnett tells us that "The world *is* a space-time continuum; all reality exists both in space and in time, and the two are indivisible. All measurements of time are really measurements in space, and conversely measurements in space depend on measurements of time" (p. 70). According to Einstein, as Barnett quotes, the nonmathematician " 'is seized by a mysterious shuddering when he hears of 'four-dimensional' things, by a feeling not unlike that awakened by thoughts of the occult. And yet there is no more commonplace statement than that the world in which we live is a four dimensional space-time continuum' " (p. 67). According to Barnett, "Once the meaning of the word 'continuum' is properly grasped Einstein's picture of the universe as a four-dimensional space-time continuum—and this is the view that underlies all modern conceptions of the universe—becomes perfectly clear. A continuum is something that is continuous. A ruler for example, is a one-dimensional space continuum" (p. 67). However, "In theory there is no reason why the steps from point to point should not be even smaller [than those normally marked on the surface of the ruler]. The distinguishing characteristic of a continuum is that the interval separating any two points may be divided into an infinite number of arbitrarily small steps" (pp. 67–68). The point is, of course, that *Slaughterhouse-Five* not only contains the literary expression or counterpart to the theory of relativity but that it is composed of a set of moments. The distance that exists between these moments is controlled by the narrator's memory and his memory does not present or recall the events of his past in a chronological fashion but rather "all at one time" in which all "moments [are] seen all at one time" (Vonnegut, p. 88). In other words, the novel creates a "true" four-dimensional space-time. The narrator's view of time, then, has no meaning, according to the theory of relativity, when it is divorced from a frame of reference. And, of course, the frame of reference in the novel is created by the narrator who defines that frame by the very act of telling his story. Time, in other words, may not be treated as an independent phenomenon divorced from the events which take place in the novel. The concept of time in *Slaughterhouse-Five* may not be the same as ours. The narrator, therefore, serves as the reader's guide to understanding the novel's concept of time in the same way that the Tralfamadorians' guide explains to them Billy's concept of time.

While Billy is a prisoner on the planet Tralfamadore he tries to explain his conception of time to the Tralfamadorians, and they are unable to understand him. Likewise, Billy cannot understand the Tralfamadorian conception of time. We are told by our narrator that "there was a lot that Billy said that was gibberish to the Tralfamadorians, too. They couldn't imagine what time looked like to him. Billy had given up on explaining that. The guide outside [the zoo Billy is in] had to explain as best he could" (p. 114). We are told by Vonnegut (our narrator) that:

> The guide invited the crowd [of Tralfamadorians] to imagine that they were looking across a desert at a mountain range on the day that was twinkling bright and clear. They could look at a peak or a bird or a cloud, at a stone right in front of them, or even down into a canyon behind them. But among them was this poor Earthling, and his head was encased in a steel sphere which he could never take off. There was only one eyehole through which he could look, and welded to that eyehole were six feet of pipe. (p. 115)

Likewise, our guide to seeing and understanding *Slaughterhouse-Five* is the narrator (or fictive "I"). We are "invited" to imagine a scene, though our scene is that of the novel itself and all that the novel presents and pictures. However, the narrator informs us that:

> This was only the beginning of Billy's miseries in the metaphor. He was also strapped to a steel lattice which was bolted to a flatcar on rails, and there was no way he could turn his head or touch the pipe. The far end of the pipe rested on a bi-pod which was

> also bolted to the flatcar. All Billy could see was the little dot at the end of the pipe. He didn't know he was on a flatcar, didn't know there was anything peculiar about his situation. (p. 115)

This passage, and the lines immediately preceding it, given above, very clearly establish the limitations of Billy's ability to understand the nature of his predicament. However, the narrator of the novel is not Billy and it is clear that these lines are intended to suggest that the narrator of the novel, like the Tralfamadorians, holds a point of view toward the physical universe which corresponds with that of the theory of relativity. Further, in a sense what we are being told is that all narration is linear and must be since that is the nature not only of the language but of literary art and yet we are also being told that conceptually things need not be this way at all—that we may structure our narration in such a way as to give the *effect* of a nonlinear, nonchronological presentation. And, of course, *Slaughterhouse-Five* is Vonnegut's attempt to produce a nonlinear, nonchronological effect. As our narrator tells us:

> Billy couldn't read Tralfamadorian, of course, but he could at least see how the books were laid out—in brief clumps of symbols separated by stars. Billy commented that the clumps might be telegrams.
> "Exactly," said the voice.
> "They *are* telegrams?"
> "There are no telegrams on Tralfamadore. But you're right: each clump of symbols is a brief, urgent message—describing a situation, a scene. We Tralfamadorians read them all at once, not one after the other. There isn't any particular relationship between all the messages, except that the author has chosen them carefully, so that, when seen all at once, they produce an image of life that is beautiful and surprising and deep. There is no beginning, no middle, no end, no suspense, no moral, no causes, no effects. What we love in our books are the depths of many marvelous moments seen all at one time." (p. 88)

Obviously, in many ways this passage suggests an internal analogy Vonnegut (as author) wishes us to make between the way in which the Tralfamadorian books are laid out and the way in which *Slaughterhouse-Five* is structured. In *Slaughterhouse-Five* each passage, like those in the Tralfamadorians' books, is an "urgent message—describing a situation, a scene." Further, there "isn't any particular relationship between all the messages [passages], except that the author has chosen them carefully." The point is, of course, that the narrator of *Slaughterhouse-Five* has chosen carefully the passages he presents but the principle of presentation is not dependent upon a chronology but rather on a relativistic and associative concept of time which grows out of the narrator's act of memory.

Time and the Structure of Reality   81

This relativistic and associative concept of time results in a nonlinear and discontinuous effect in the structuring of the novel.

The narrator has told us that Billy Pilgrim *"has come unstuck in time"* (p. 22). And, though Billy is able to "re-live" his past and his future, he can see only one event at a time and his concept of time is linear. The Tralfamadorians, on the other hand, experience all time as existing simultaneously and as being fatalistically determined. The explanation the Tralfamadorians give Billy about the end of the universe explains their concept of time. " 'We [the Tralfamadorians] blow it up, experimenting with new fuels for our flying saucers. A Tralfamadorian test pilot presses a starter button, and the whole Universe disappears.' So it goes" (p. 117). Billy, however, questions, " 'If you know this,' said Billy, 'isn't there some way you can prevent it? Can't you keep the pilot from *pressing* the button?' " and Billy is told that " 'He [the test pilot] has *always* pressed it, and he always *will*. We *always* let him and we always *will* let him. The moment is *structured* that way' " (p. 117).

The novel, too, is "structured that way"; the various moments which make up *Slaughterhouse-Five* are structured the way they are to give the effect of occurring simultaneously. The actual presentation of the various passages (moments) in the novel may give the *appearance* of a continuum but their effect conceptually is to break or explode this continuum and thereby suggest a discontinuous universe rather than a continuous one.

We will see in the following pages that "Chapter One" is not only the beginning of the novel but also, conceptually, its end. And, as such, it provides a structural analogy to the Tralfamadorians' concept of time which suggests that the beginning, middle, and end exist simultaneously. In this first chapter Vonnegut (as narrator) is engaged in the act of recording through the device of his memory a series of moments which encapsule pertinent information about his attempts to write a book about Dresden.

We learn that the narrator "as a trafficker in climaxes and thrills and characterization and wonderful dialogue and suspense and confrontations . . . had outlined the Dresden story many times. The best outlines . . . [he] ever made, or anyway the prettiest one, [were] on the back of a roll of wallpaper" (p. 5). In short, the narrator is a writer (author) who describes the processes or methods of his writing—their success and failure—and, obviously the ones he describes in the opening pages of the novel are the ones which have failed. As Robbe-Grillet points out, "A novel which is no more than the grammatical example illustrating a rule—even accompanied by its exception—would naturally be useless: the statement of the rule would suffice" (p. 13). We are informed by the narrator that he:

used . . . [his] daughter's crayons, a different color for each main character. One end of the wallpaper was the beginning of the story, and the other end was at the end, and then there was all that middle part, which was the middle. And the blue line met the red line and then the yellow line, and the yellow line stopped because the character represented by the yellow line was dead. And so on. The destruction of Dresden was represented by a vertical band of orange crosshatching, and all the lines that were still alive passed through it, came out the other side. (p. 5)

In quick succession we learn that the narrator was a student at "the University of Chicago for a while after the Second World War," that in a conversation with his father he was told "you know—you never wrote a story with a villain in it," and that "one of the things . . . [he] learned in college after the war was that there weren't any villains" (p. 8). This rather matter-of-fact confession (tongue in cheek) about the lack of villains, however, is obviously false. The novel does have its villains, and the narrator does believe in them in spite of what he has "learned in college." Immediately following this passage in the novel another occurs which relates an experience the narrator had while "studying to be an anthropologist" (p. 8). We are told that he "was . . . working as a police reporter for the famous Chicago City News Bureau for twenty-eight dollars a week" and that he "worked sixteen hours straight" at one time (p. 8). He informs us that:

On the first story . . . [he] covered . . . [he] had to dictate over the telephone to one of those beastly girls. It was about a young veteran who had taken a job running an old fashioned elevator in an office building. The elevator door on the first floor was ornamental iron lace. Iron ivy snaked in and out of the holes. There was an iron twig with two iron lovebirds perched upon it. (p. 9)

The purpose of this description of the elevator is, of course, to prepare us for the irony of the young veteran's death. Vonnegut tells us after a rather matter-of-fact description of the method by which news stories were telephoned in that:

This veteran decided to take his car into the basement, and he closed the door and started down, but his wedding ring was caught in all the ornaments. So he was hoisted into the air and the floor of the car went down, dropped out from under him, and the top of the car squashed him. So it goes. (p. 9)

Throughout the opening chapter, as well as throughout the novel, this type of description is just one of several techniques the narrator uses to convey his point—that the fire-bombing of Dresden was a slaughter and served no useful military purpose. The technique he uses is to personalize, through his own experience, the impersonal, to humanize the inhumane. While it may be "easy" to understand the death (tragic or otherwise) of a single human being, the question which haunts the narrator is how to convey the sense of slaughter of such magnitude when a slaughter is by its very nature impersonal. The narrator's answer is to make use of his own personal experiences, not only in the Second World War but in life, to understand the fire-bombing of Dresden. Immediately following the incident of the veteran's death our narrator informs us that:

> Even then I was supposedly writing a book about Dresden. It wasn't a famous air raid back then in America. Not many Americans knew how much worse it had been than Hiroshima, for instance. I didn't know that, either. There hadn't been much publicity. (p. 10)

The initial conception for *Slaughterhouse-Five*, then, lies in the narrator's memory of having lived through the fire-bombing of Dresden. Yet at the time he was a prisoner in Dresden the total impact of what he was involved in did not reach him. It is only after the war that he finally came, through the aid of his memory and inquiry into the military purpose of the fire-bombing, to understand the significance of the events he witnessed.

In "Chapter One" we learn that in an attempt to "jog" his memory our fictional narrator Vonnegut decides to look up an old war buddy of his by the name of Bernard V. O'Hare:

> When I was somewhat younger, working on my famous Dresden book, I asked an old war buddy named Bernard V. O'Hare if I could come to see him. He was a district attorney in Pennsylvania. I was a writer in Cape Cod. We had been privates in the war, infantry scouts. We had never expected to make any money after the war, but we were doing quite well.
> I had the Bell Telephone Company find him for me. They are wonderful that way. I have this disease late at night sometimes, involving alcohol and the telephone company. I get drunk, and I drive my wife away with a breath like mustard gas and roses. And then, speaking gravely and elegantly into the telephone, I ask the telephone operator to connect me with this friend or that one, from whom I have not heard in years. (p. 4)

Vonnegut, our fictional narrator, finally is able to reach O'Hare on the telephone and explains to him " 'Listen—' I said, 'I'm writing this book about Dresden. I'd like some help remembering stuff. I wonder if I could come down and see you, and we could drink and talk and remember' " (p. 4). O'Hare tells the narrator that "he . . . [can't] remember much" but "to come ahead" anyway (p. 4). These remarks are followed immediately by others about Vonnegut's view of how the "climax of the book" will be "the execution of poor old Edgar Derby" (p. 5). He tells us that:

> the irony is *so* great. A whole city gets burned down, and thousands and thousands of people are killed. And then this one American foot soldier is arrested in the ruins for taking a teapot. And he's given a regular trial, and then he's shot by a firing squad. (p. 5)

Slaughterhouse-Five does end with this climax but it is somewhat overshadowed by a more important idea—that out of death comes life. Nevertheless, it is out of this incident—Vonnegut's telephone conversation with O'Hare—that the alternate title to the novel comes. We are told that "A couple of weeks after . . . [he] really *did* go see him. . . ."

> That must have been in 1964 or so—whatever the last year was for the New York World's Fair. Eheu, *fugaces labuntur anni*. My name is Yon Yonson. There was a young man from Stamboul.
> I took two little girls with me, my daughter, Nanny, and her best friend, Allison Mitchell. They had never been off Cape Cod before. (p. 11)

Finally, he arrives at O'Hare's house, knocks on the door, meets O'Hare's "nice" wife "to whom this book is dedicated," and discovers that "Mary didn't like me or didn't like *something* about the night. She was polite but chilly" (p. 12). The reason Mary O'Hare reacts the way she does is because she fears that Vonnegut will glorify the war rather than convey its horror. We learn from Vonnegut that Mary felt "Well, *I* know, . . . You'll be played in the movies by Frank Sinatra and John Wayne or some of those other glamorous, war-loving, dirty old men. And war will look just wonderful, so we'll have a lot more of them. And they'll be fought by babies like the babies upstairs [Vonnegut's daughter, her friend Allison Mitchell, and Mary O'Hare's children]" (p. 14). Vonnegut has already informed us that "We [he and others] *had* been foolish virgins in the war, right at the end of childhood" (p. 14). As a consequence of Mary's remarks, the narrator informs us "So then I understood. It was war that made her [Mary] so angry. She didn't want her babies or anybody else's babies killed in wars. And she thought wars were partly encouraged by books and movies" (p. 15). The result of his realization is a pledge he makes to Mary:

> So I held up my right hand and I made her a promise: "Mary," I said, "I don't think this book of mine is ever going to be finished. I must have written five thousand pages by now, and thrown them all away. If I ever do finish it, though, I give you my word of honor: there won't be a part for Frank Sinatra or John Wayne."
> "I tell you what," I said, "I'll call it *The Children's Crusade*."
> She was my friend after that. (p. 15)

Time and the Structure of Reality   85

This promise to Mary results in Vonnegut's and O'Hare's curiosity being aroused about "the real Children's Crusade, so O'Hare looked it up in a book he had, *Extraordinary Popular Delusions and the Madness of Crowds*, by Charles Mackay, LL.D. It was first published in London in 1841" (p. 15). We are quickly told by O'Hare, who reads from Mackay's volume, that "history in her solemn page informs us that the crusaders were but ignorant and savage men, that their pathway was one of blood and tears" (p. 15). Further, we learn that "the Children's Crusade started in 1213, when two monks got the idea of raising armies of children in Germany and France, and selling them in North Africa as slaves. Thirty thousand children volunteered, thinking they were going to Palestine" (p. 16). O'Hare's reading of Mackay's volume quickly ends and Vonnegut comments:

> I slept that night in one of the children's bedrooms. O'Hare had put a book for me on the bedside table. It was *Dresden, History, Stage* and *Gallery*, by Mary Endell. It was published in 1908, and its introduction began: *It is hoped that this little book will make itself useful. It attempts to give to an English-reading public a bird's-eye view of how Dresden came to look as it does.* (p. 17)

Endell's book not only treats the architectural and cultural genius that *was* Dresden but, in its history, outlines the Prussian destruction of Dresden in 1760. The function in *Slaughterhouse-Five* of referring to these two works as well as to others—*Valley of the Dolls, The Bombing of Dresden, The Execution of Private Slovik, The Red Badge of Courage*, and the imaginary *Maniacs in the Fourth Dimension* by Kilgore Trout—is to attempt to establish a sense of distance between the narrator and his own memory of the fire-bombing of Dresden. At the same time, these references to history serve another function and that function is to try to aid the reader in coming to grips with understanding the slaughter that took place in Dresden. Not only do these works suggest that destruction and tragedy have been a part of our history but that they will continue to be a part of our future history. Earlier in "Chapter One" our narrator informs us that "Over the years, people I've met have often asked me what I'm working on, and I've usually replied that the main thing was a book about Dresden. I said that to Harrison Starr, the movie-maker, one time, and he raised his eyebrows and inquired, 'Is it an anti-war book?' " and Vonnegut as fictional narrator replies, "Yes" (p. 3). In the sentence following we learn that:

> "You know what I say to people when I hear they're writing anti-war books?"
> "No. What do you say Harrison Starr?"

"I say, 'Why don't you write an anti-*glacier* book instead?' "
What he meant, of course, was that there would always be wars, that they were as easy to stop as glaciers. I believe that, too. (p. 3)

Vonnegut's attitude may be somewhat pessimistic but, nevertheless, it is also clear that he feels morally committed to write his book. Other references to history and books from the past include Erika Ostrovsky's *Celine and His Vision* and the *Gideon Bible*. The latter reference provides Vonnegut a way of getting out of "Chapter One" and concluding his memories about previous attempts he has made to write *Slaughterhouse-Five*. The occasion is provided by his return trip to Dresden with O'Hare. We are told by Vonnegut that "there was a Lufthansa plane that was supposed to fly from Boston to Frankfurt. O'Hare was supposed to get on in Philadelphia and I was supposed to get on in Boston, and off we'd go. But Boston was socked in, so the plane flew straight to Frankfurt from Philadelphia" (p. 20). "Lufthansa," we are told, "put . . . [Vonnegut] in a limousine with some other non-persons and sent us to a motel for a non-night" (p. 20). Once in his motel room Vonnegut examines briefly Theodore Roethke's *Words for the Wind* and Ostrovsky's book on Celine. His attention turns, however, to a copy of the *Gideon Bible* "for tales of great destruction" (p. 21). What he finds, of course, is the story of Sodom and Gomorrah:

> I looked through the Gideon Bible in my motel room for tales of great destruction. *The sun was risen upon the Earth when Lot entered into Zo-ar,* I read. *Then the Lord rained upon Sodom and upon Gomorrah brimstone and fire from the Lord out of Heaven; and He overthrew those cities, and all the plain, and all the inhabitants of the cities, and that which grew upon the ground.*
> So it goes.
> Those were vile people in both those cities, as is well known. The world was better off without them.
> And Lot's wife, of course, was told not to look back where all those people and their homes had been. But she *did* look back, and I love her for that, because it was so human.
> So she turned to a pillar of salt. So it goes. (pp. 21–22)

In its immediate context this passage provides the *raison d'être* for the inner story the narrator creates about Billy Pilgrim. It also provides a justification or rationalization (or both) for Vonnegut's statements and explanations about his many previous attempts to write *Slaughterhouse-Five* and it does so since it emphasizes the major concern of the narrator—his desire to be, like Lot's wife, "human." The irony of the passage, however, is that as Lot's wife was "turned to a pillar of salt" by looking back at "where all those people and their homes had been," so too,

Vonnegut will turn into "a pillar of salt." From another point of view, this passage suggests that what we are about to read in "Chapter Two," and throughout the novel, about Billy Pilgrim, is a way of looking back—that what follows from this point in "Chapter One" is an allegory and this allegory will provide the reader with a way of treating Dresden without becoming a pillar of salt before he is able to accomplish his goal. The above passage, however, is only the penultimate "moment" of "Chapter One," for its application in a sense follows immediately. Vonnegut declares:

> People aren't supposed to look back. I'm certainly not going to do it anymore.
> I've finished my war book now. The next one I write is going to be fun.
> This one is a failure, and had to be, since it was written by a pillar of salt. It begins like this:
> *Listen:*
> *Billy Pilgrim has come unstuck in time.*
> *It ends like this:*
> Poo-tee-weet? (p. 22)

With this passage "Chapter One" comes to an end. From one point of view what we have been told is that conceptually "Chapter One" is not only the beginning of the novel but also its end. What remains is the allegory itself, which comprises the remaining nine chapters of *Slaughterhouse-Five*. In other words, "Chapter One" not only provides the *raison d'être* for what follows in the novel but it also provides an explanation for the novel after the fact of the novel's accomplishment. The ending of the novel—the *"Poo-tee-weet?"* of "Chapter Ten"—rather than providing an answer to what has been presented in the novel, or will be presented in the novel from this point on, only raises a question. For we learn at the very end that "One bird said to Billy Pilgrim, *'Poo-tee-weet?'*" (p. 215). The bird's song which Billy hears occurs in the middle of the "corpse mines" which was Dresden. Dresden, after the fire-bombing, has become one vast cemetery in which the few remaining survivors have given up trying to dig out the buried. The bird's song suggests and symbolizes life, its affirmation, and more importantly, its possibilities (hopes) for a future without war. Yet the bird's song ends with a question mark and this raises the question "Are we going to affirm life or are we going to choose, instead, death and other Dresdens?" And, as we have seen in *The Einstein Intersection*, "Endings to be useful must be inconclusive."[13]

Slaughterhouse-Five, though it may have its initial conception in the fire-bombing of Dresden, is not simply an anti-war book. For, from another point of view, the annihilation of Dresden provides the subject for a greater theme whose subject is life. In "Chapter One" Vonnegut's major subject is a preoccupation with the problems of his art. Almost all of this chapter is devoted to a discussion or explanation of the narrator's attempts, as he recalls them, to write a novel about Dresden. But in becoming preoccupied with this problem, he learns a greater lesson which is that the novel has, at its very limits, the subject of fiction itself. Robbe-Grillet suggests that "the function of art is never to illustrate a truth—or even an interrogation—known in advance, but to bring into the world certain interrogations (and also, perhaps, in time, certain answers) not yet known as such to themselves" (p. 14). Further, Robbe-Grillet suggests that "when we ask [the novelist] why he has written his book, he has only one answer: To try and find out why I wanted to write it" (p. 14). We also learn, as Robbe-Grillet suggests, that "what constitutes the novelist's strength is precisely that he invents, that he invents quite freely, without a model. The remarkable thing about modern fiction is that it asserts this characteristic quite deliberately, to such a degree that invention and imagination become, at the limit, the very subject of the book" (p. 32). In "Chapter One" we have Vonnegut's investigation of his own memory and the problems of his art and his inability to find a satisfactory way of presenting the slaughter of 135,000 human beings. What I am suggesting is that memory remains for Vonnegut his best weapon but that in the very act of presenting that memory in the novel it becomes hopelessly inadequate. In other words, the process of memory remains and provides, in its broad outlines, the means by which it will cancel itself out and, therefore, lead to other memories, and so forth, throughout the novel. Another way of stating this is to say that the outline the narrator tells us about early in "Chapter One" fails. The reason it fails is because it describes a method which is not realized in the novel; it describes only the way in which other novels have been written either in the past by the narrator or by someone else. This outline incorporates a linear or chronological (historical) presentation of events and incidents in a series. The use of the outline, then, presupposes that the memory will reproduce the past as it actually occurred, that it will present things in a chronological fashion. And the failure of Vonnegut's (the narrator's) outline to be completed in a book illustrates the failure of the use of the Newtonian concept of time to structure a novel based on a twentieth-century relativistic worldview.

In summary, our apprehension of time in *Slaughterhouse-Five* has been dependent upon the narrator's perception of the nature of the universe and reality. The narrative technique of the novel has been to present time as a series of discontinuous moments, each complete in its duration, but existing, simultaneously, in a discontinuous universe. The form of the novel, then, has been seen to be entirely appropriate to its world view, both implicitly and explicitly within the novel. The narrator, in structuring his novel to show his relativistic and discontinuous world-view, has become a literary mathematician.

As David Daiches suggests in *The Novel and the Modern World,* the new concept of time "led to a suspicion of the old kind of plot which carried characters forward from moment to moment in a precise chronological sequence, and there developed instead the kind of narrative texture that moved backward and forward with a new freedom to try to capture the sense of time as it actually operates in the human awareness of it."[14] But, what Vonnegut has added to this view of time is the idea that our sense of time itself has changed and should, therefore, be reflected in the structure of the modern novel. The very complexity of the devices he uses, and his obvious understanding of them, suggests that, finally, he along with a select group of other writers (Delany, Aldiss, Brunner, etc.) has brought, at long last, a concern for craft to science fiction. The result is the emergence, as Judith Merill suggests, of a literature that is "more radical and more exciting—intellectually *and* artistically—. . . than anything up till now" and that "it holds the promise of an entire new literature."[15]

5

A Wholistic Theory of the Science-Fiction Novel

A German proverb says, "Alle Vergleiche hinken"—all analogies limp. One must bear this in mind whenever the temptation arises to regard an analogy as proof—to jump to the conclusion that if neutrinos exist, then ghosts must exist.

On the other hand, it seems perfectly legitimate, and even imperative, to assimilate into our habits of thought the lessons that modern physics has taught us, and to incorporate them into our world view. Relativity and quantum theory are transforming man's image of the universe around him radically, but the dogmas of nineteenth-century science still dominate the habits of thought of the average educated person who prides himself on a 'radical' outlook.

Arthur Koestler, *"Order from Disorder"*

Organic theories of art are based on the idea of an analogy. That analogy most often finds its expression in terms of the metaphor that a literary work of art is *like* a biological organism—a plant, for instance. Yet somehow this metaphor seems inadequate to express the developments which have taken place in the art of the science-fiction novel. Geoffrey Hartman in "Structuralism: the Anglo-American Adventure" points out that the

> word "organicism" is seen to stand for the fact that the whole is greater than its parts, and that the whole is a system. A dream, a plant, a work of art, a machine, are all systems; the common factor being that they separate, ecologically, what is "outside" from what is "inside," and so impose, within limits, their form on whatever passes into them. (p. 147)

Hartman also suggests that there has always been "an organic postulate of this kind, at least since Coleridge" (p. 147). Further, he declares that:

> organic form is . . . a more difficult concept to apply to art [than other theories], for the organic seems always in touch with the origin, instead of having to seek it by one fateful method. In nature there is no Single Way except what leads to death; and as long as the organism can modify itself, that is, change its ways, it avoids death. Seed becomes petal, petal blossom, blossom fruit, fruit seed. (pp. 149–50)

Superficially, this view of organic form seems sound enough. Yet upon closer examination it is found wanting in the face of modern science. Hartman declares that "spatial form (field theory) . . . seems to deny the very idea of origin, to the point where nothing is 'here and now' yet everything 'there' " (p. 150). What Hartman is suggesting is that organicism conceptually takes its formulation from a certain view of nature which is no longer particularly reliable or accurate in its description of the universe. For instance, obviously, in the passage quoted above the analogy between form and plant does not take into account mutation (genetic) or the fact that all life-forms are open systems which must receive energy from the outside in order to maintain their cycle of reproduction and growth. Further, this formulation of an organic form implicitly contains the assumption that nature operates in terms of a strict causality since "seed becomes petal, petal blossom, blossom fruit, fruit seed" ad infinitum. In the face of modern science's view of the universe and, consequently, nature, nothing could be further from the truth. Arthur Koestler explains in his essay "Order from Disorder" that in

> biology, too, [in comparison to physics], there is a search for new principles—or, perhaps, a revival of earlier insights—which would provide a more satisfactory approach to the creative aspects of evolution than Neo-Darwinism, for all its historical merits, has been able to provide. The claim that chance mutations preserved by natural selection provide the *complete* explanation of the emergence of higher forms of life and its complex, purposive forms of behavior may turn out to be the swan song of a presumptuous generation of biologists. There is today a growing number of eminent biologists who have come to realize that chance mutations may provide part of the explanation, but not the whole explanation, and perhaps not even an important part of it.[1]

Koestler continues, however, by pointing out that there are "no completely isolated systems . . . known even in inanimate nature; all living organisms are 'open systems' which absorb energy and matter from their environment" (p. 64). Rene Wellek in *Concepts of Criticism* suggests that "in spite of the basic truth of the insight of organicism, the unity of content and form, we have arrived today at something like a deadend."[2]

It would seem, then, that Hartman, Koestler, and Wellek all perceive the limitations of organicism in explaining the fundamentals of the universe and art. I would like to suggest that organicism is a product or result of a certain way of looking at nature and that if our view of nature changes, so too must our theories of literary art.

In proposing a wholistic theory of the science-fiction novel, in its broad outline, I do not reject the organic theory but rather I suggest that this theory is a special argument or case within a more general theory of the novel which must now take into account the various principles of modern mathematical physics we have previously discussed. For it is clear, as Koestler suggests in the introductory passage to this chapter, that the philosophical implications of the theory of relativity, of quantum mechanics, and the recent developments which have taken place in mathematics have transformed the way in which man sees his universe.

Wholistic theories of art are not new and, at the risk of committing the generic fallacy, we may discover their origins in Aristotle's *Physics*. William K. Wimsatt, Jr. and Cleanth Brooks point out in their *Literary Criticism: A Short History* that Aristotle defined the whole as

> that from which nothing is wanting, as a whole man or a whole box . . . "whole" and "complete" are either quite identical or closely akin. Nothing is complete (teleion) which has no end (telos); and the end is a limit.[3]

This definition of the "whole," however, must now be changed or modified to take into account a different conception of the universe. For modern works of fiction are not closed or complete in Aristotle's sense, but exhibit a certain openness or indeterminacy of form. And, as Arthur Koestler suggests:

> The scientific revolution of the seventeenth century put a temporary end to this holistic view [that view "that everything in the universe hangs together, partly by mechanical causes but mainly by hidden affinities"] and proclaimed mechanical causality as the absolute ruler of matter and mind. Now we are witnessing a swing of the pendulum in the opposite direction. The twin tyranny of mechanical causality and strict determinism has come to an end; the universe has acquired a new look, which seems to reflect some ancient, archetypal intuitions of unity-in-diversity, on a higher turn of the spiral. (p. 60)

The scientific revolution of the seventeenth century seems to have curtailed the organic development of the novel until the overthrow of classical mechanics became a reality. The Romantics, in their poetry, seem to have rebelled against the mechanistic philosophy of the seventeenth and eighteenth centuries while the novel seems to have gone in the other direction. And, as I pointed out in chapter 1, the science-fiction novel seems to have paralleled in its development the novel as a whole while recapitulating that development in something less than one hundred years. What is at issue, however, is a different way of understanding what we mean by the "whole." In the Aristotelian definition given above and within the seventeenth century's view of the universe, "the underlying concept of the whole is based on the idea of a strict causality; that is, the whole is based on a causal interrelation of its parts—a beginning, middle, and end—which gives rise to a unity or oneness" (Wimsatt, pp. 30–32). In the new view, as Koestler suggests, "the whole is as necessary for the understanding of its parts as the part is for the understanding of the whole. In biology this trend is again obvious; in physics it is fairly recent and fraught with revolutionary implications" (p. 57). Our conception, then, of the "whole" must change if we are to take into account the indirect implications of modern science for the form of the science-fiction novel. In the view which I am suggesting we can no longer separate out the parts from a whole; that is, what we call a part is in actual fact the result or product of its interaction with its surroundings. This view, as I have suggested elsewhere in this work, is the result, albeit indirectly, of relativity and quantum theory. The point is, again as Koestler suggests, that it is "impossible to separate any part of the universe from the rest" (p. 57). Likewise, it is impossible to separate any part of the novel from the rest.

The distinction between organic and wholistic is dependent upon how these two words are related to the terms metaphor and model. In brief, I have argued throughout my discussion that one of the characteristics of the modern science-fiction novel is that it is no longer structured in terms of a series of metaphors which present a picture *of* nature but rather that the science-fiction novel is structured in terms of a set of principles which constitute a model and this model determines the novel's form. For instance, in chapter 3 I demonstrated that the principles of probability theory constitute a model which describes the world of the novel *Report on Probability A*. In the eighteenth- and nineteenth-century novel, however, the organic analogies (metaphors) which existed in the novel functioned in a structure which was the result of a mechanistic, Newtonian, causal world view and reflected man's view *of* nature rather than his *relation to* nature. I am applying the term wholistic, then, to that novel which is based on a set of principles taken from modern science and which presents a picture of our *relation* to nature rather than presents a picture *of* nature.

The distinction between organic and wholistic is crucial and presupposes a different way, perhaps, of achieving much the same end; that is, modern science returns us, in a sense, to an earlier conception of holism which existed in art before the scientific revolution of the seventeenth century, but it does so from a radically different set of premises and starting points. And it is, of course, these different starting points and premises that I have been interested in throughout my examination of the science-fiction novel. The distinction, then, is not simply a quarrel between how we define two words—organic and wholistic—but resides in an altered way of looking at the novel and the universe. Theoretically, this relationship may, perhaps, be better understood by an analogy. For instance, an organic theory of literary art bears the same relationship to a wholistic theory as does Newtonian physics to the theory of relativity. A wholistic theory does not reject the organic but simply states that it is a limited and somewhat special case within a more encompassing theory of the novel. Consequently, the three novels I have examined—*The Einstein Intersection, Report on Probability A,* and *Slaughterhouse-Five*—are organic novels and they are also wholistic. In the analogy I have given above between an organic-wholistic theory of the novel and a Newtonian-Einsteinian one, I do not mean to suggest that the principles of relativity are necessarily the only principles which determine what a wholistic theory is or should be. Obviously, modern mathematics and quantum theory each contribute to the formulation of this wholistic theory and how we should understand it. And, further, it should be obvious that the formulation of a critical theory of the novel will arise out of our observation of fundamental changes which have taken place in the form and structure of the novel. What I would see in this new theory of the novel and nature, then, is an ultimate fusion of science with literary art and literary criticism. For it should be clear that the relationship of literary art and criticism to modern science, though indirect, is becoming increasingly interfacial. However, a word of caution is, perhaps, necessary.

In *Intelligence in the Modern World* John Dewey cautions that "educational science cannot be constructed simply by borrowing the techniques of experiment and measurement found in physical science."[4] Likewise, in paraphrase of Dewey, I would suggest that a science of literature may not be created simply by borrowing the techniques of science and applying them to the study of literary art. In part, the problem of creating a science of literature resides in what we mean by science. Obviously if we restrict science to "the term mathematics," as Dewey suggests, "or to disciplines in which exact results can be determined by rigorous methods of demonstration," then, "such a conception limits even the claims of physics and chemistry to be sciences, for according to it [the view that mathematics is the only true science] the only scientific portion of these subjects is the strictly mathematical" (p. 631). Further, Dewey points out:

> The position of what are ordinarily termed the biological sciences is even more dubious, while social subjects and psychology would hardly rank as sciences at all, when measured by this definition. Clearly we must take the idea of science with some latitude. We must take it with sufficient looseness to include all the subjects that are usually regarded as sciences. The important thing is to discover those traits in virtue of which various fields are called scientific. When we raise the question in this way, we are led to put emphasis upon *methods* of dealing with the subject-matter rather than to look for uniform objective traits in subject-matter. From this point of view, science signifies, I take it, the existence of systematic methods of inquiry, which when they are brought to bear on a range of facts, enable us to understand them better and to control them more intelligently, less haphazardly and with less routine. (pp. 631–32)

The significant phrase in the above passage is "the existence of systematic methods of inquiry" for, as I pointed out in chapter 1, Edgar Stanley Hyman has argued that the power of modern literary criticism derives from the fact that it is an "organized use of non-literary techniques and bodies of knowledge to obtain insights into literature" and that these bodies of knowledge are those of science. In support of this contention, Hyman points out that "among the methods and disciplines that have been established as useful for literary criticism, the social sciences come to mind first, a reservoir so vast that it has hardly yet been tapped" (p. 5). Hyman suggests:

> From psychoanalysis critics have borrowed the basic assumptions of the operations of the subconscious mind, demonstrating its deeper "wishes" through associations and "clusters" of images; the basic mechanisms of dream-distortion, such as condensation, displacement, and splitting, which are also the basic mechanisms of poetic-formation; the Jungian concept of archetypes, and much else. They have taken the concept of "configurations" from the gestaltists; basic experimental data about animal and child behavior from the laboratory psychologists; information about the pathological expressions of the human mind from the clinical psychologists; discoveries about the behavior of man in groups and social patterns from the social psychologists; and a great deal more, from Jaensch's "eidetic images" and similarly purely subjective material to the most objective physical and chemical data reported by neurology and endochrinological psychologies. (p. 5)

Obviously, if we accept Dewey's view of science, then, the social sciences are sciences. Further, Hyman declares:

> In addition to the social sciences, a number of other modern disciplines have been very fruitful, or are potentially so. Literary scholarship, although hardly a new field, has by our century accumulated so great a body of accurate information and so exact a body of procedures that with the addition of critical imagination it has been made to produce a type of scholarly criticism completely 'modern' in the sense used above ... The traditional scholarly areas of linguistics and philology, with the addition of the modern field of semantics, have opened up to criticism enormous vistas, only slightly explored. The physical and biological sciences have provided criticism with

such basic ingredients as the experimental method itself, as well as theories of great metaphoric usefulness, like "evolution" and modern physical "relativity," "field," and "indeterminacy" concepts. . . . Besides these bodies of theory and knowledge, modern criticism has developed a number of specialized procedures of its own and methodized them, sometimes on the analogy of scientific procedure. Such are the pursuits of biographical information, the exploration of ambiguities, the study of symbolic action and communication in literary works [communication theory], and close reading, hard work, and detailed exploration of texts in general. (p. 6)

There can be no question, then, that modern literary criticism has "borrowed" and systematically made use of areas of non-literary knowledge. Our understanding of science and what we mean by that word is no longer limited simply to mathematics. This is one of the fundamental differences between the science of the nineteenth century and that of today. And as J. Bronowski suggests in "The Discovery of Form":

The common reader is accustomed to think of science as the pursuit of facts: and the more exact the facts, the more scientific he feels them to be. This is the picture of science which was created in the public mind by the researchers of the last century. It was put into words most pointedly by one of the giants of mathematical physics in that age, Lord Kelvin, in two sentences which are still quoted as gospel. 'If you can measure that of which you speak, and can express it by a number, you know something of your subject. If you cannot measure it, your knowledge is meagre and unsatisfactory!' (p. 3)

Bronowski further tells us that "the aim of science, we now see, is to find the relations which give order to this raw material, the shapes and structures in which the measurements fit" (p. 3). The borrowing of techniques and methods from the sciences does not constitute a science, if we conceive of science in the narrow sense of mathematics or measurement. However, if by science we understand an organized and systematic use of various concepts which we apply to the study of literary art, then, these concepts become the basic principles for a science of literature. The fact that certain ideas and concepts first appeared in mathematical physics does not diminish their significance or prevent their incorporation into literary criticism. Rather, quite the contrary is indicated. As the novel becomes increasingly sophisticated in its structure and form and as it incorporates increasingly the principles, concepts, and ideas of modern science into its form and structure, we must expect that we will be forced to develop new procedures and methods of examination in our study of the novel. For underlying all developments in the sciences—the social sciences, biology, psychology, etc.—there exists, apparently, a fundamental set of principles and these principles have their first formulation and understanding in modern mathematical physics. A wholistic theory of the science-fiction novel, then, constitutes nothing more than a recognition that the science-fiction novel must take into account the various principles and concepts of science which exist within it. In other words, the novel creates within itself a model, and this model consists of a set of "rules" which define the limits and boundaries of the novel as a fictional system. These rules may define the nature of not only the physical world presented in the novel, that is, its world view, but also must take into account the presence of man in that world. And, of course, different novels will result in different models, though all these models will share certain characteristics, certain principles, with each other.

I suggested at the end of chapter 1 that science fiction creates a nonexistent reality, a reality which has existence only as a fictional system or product of the imagination. In the nineteenth century's view of science it was assumed that science by way of measurement was becoming increasingly accurate in its description of reality. Thomas D. Clareson in "The Other Side of Realism" discusses the inappropriateness of "naturalism transferred to science fiction," and cites James B. Conant who "makes an analogy between the scientists of the period [the nineteenth century] and the 'early explorers and map makers.' "[5] Clareson quotes Conant to the effect that:

> by a series of successive approximations, so to speak, maps and descriptions of distant lands were becoming closer and closer *to accurate descriptions of reality*. Why should not the labors of those who worked in the laboratories have the same outcome? No one doubted that there were real rivers, mountains, trees, bays with tides, rainfall, snowfall, glaciers; one could doubt any particular map or description, of course, but given time and patience, *it was assumed the truth would be ascertained*. By the same token there must be a *truth* about the nature of heat, light, and matter. (p. 5)

The point is, as Clareson points out, that "in capping his assertion of the weakness of the 'in principle' theory, Conant sets up an island surrounded by reefs and that made direct access out of the question except with special equipment" (p. 6). Further, we are told:

> The geographer-sea captain who came upon the island could gaze at it lovingly with his telescope and make certain approximations; he knew that when he returned with the necessary equipment, he would reach the island, map every foot of its surface, and learn all that could be known of it. He would know it in its fullest reality. (p. 5)

If science in the nineteenth century held the belief that reality could be made known through "a series of successive approximations," aided "with the necessary equipment," so too, the novelist thought he could picture life as it really was. Clareson tells us that William Dean Howells held that "truth to life is the supreme office of the novel, in whatever form . . . the business of the novelist is to make you *understand the real world through his faithful effigy to it*" (p. 6). And, according to Clareson, "The novelist with his faithful, representational effigy; the scientist with his inexorable physical analysis: so they described the reality of the world" (pp. 6–7). Literary realism and naturalism may have been, in one sense, a reaction against "the threat of nihilism incipient in the newly-emphasized concept of a mechanistic universe" but, it may also be argued, though in a different sense, that this very realism-naturalism, in its attempt to describe the world representationally and to picture life in literary art as it actually was, involved a similar, if not identical, concept of reality as the one which the scientist attempted to "capture" or map through the aid of his "special equipment" (Clareson, p. 9). Reality, to the eighteenth- and nineteenth-century scientific mind was discoverable and, therefore, knowable. This view of reality, as Susan Sontag points out in "Against Interpretation," "which most artists and critics have discarded," stands in stark contrast to the view which modern physics holds. Sontag also suggests that these same (modern) artists and critics have also replaced "the theory of art as representation of an outer reality in favor of the theory of art as subjective expression" (p. 153). On the other hand, Clareson tells us that "any writer, however bizarre his imagined world, has to make that world sufficiently representational to be acceptable by his reader" (p. 3). The paradox which seems to arise from these two conflicting points of view, however, is not insurmountable. In the modern view, the view Sontag gives, the modern artists have not rejected or discarded representation as a theory of literary art per se. Rather, the modern artists and critics have simply stated that they have rejected that theory of representation which links the world of the novel to an outer reality. What the modern novel presents, then, is a representation of its own reality. Yet, since the novel must be "sufficiently representational to be acceptable by the reader," and I might also add, be intelligible to that reader, the novel must share a set of common elements between present reality (our reality) and the reality created by the novel—whether that reality be past, present, or future—and which has existence within the novel. In other words, to use an analogy, one assumption of all criticism which examines the literature of the past is that it presupposes, in a very basic sense, that the nature of our language has not changed so much that we can no longer understand the ancients. Now, if we reverse this analogy, we may assume that the literature of the future (which still has to be written) will be understandable because its language and understanding of us will be, in part, based on our own language. For example, this problem is clearly and implicitly formulated in Anthony Burgess's *A Clockwork Orange*. The novel is set in the immediate future. Burgess creates a language for this future which is a mixture of English and Russian. And, as Stanley Edgar Hyman points out in his "Afterword" to *A Clockwork Orange:*

> At first the vocabulary seems incomprehensible: "you could peet it with vellocet or synthemesc or drencrom or one or two other vesches." Then the reader, even if he knows no Russian discovers that some of the meaning is clear from context: "to tolchock some old veck in an alley and viddy him swim in his blood."[6]

The point is that languages evolve or develop along certain apparently "discoverable" lines and by projecting or extrapolating those lines (principles) we may create a possible language of the future which is still understandable and intelligible to use, though, of course, it will not be so at all points. Consequently, the science-fiction novel may create a nonexistent reality which is no longer representational in terms of an outer reality simply because what constitutes an outer reality for us will not be the same as that which constitutes an outer reality for the future. Further, the past (our past) does not constitute our reality but only contributes to it. Likewise, the present (our present) becomes a past when understood in the face of a future reality. The point is, of course, that this line of reasoning can only be "pushed" so far before it breaks down. Obviously, few readers would be interested in learning an entirely new language in order to read a novel of problematical value. Further, I should point out that this line of reasoning presupposes the acceptance of a *fiction;* that is, that the science-fiction novel may create a future. If we accept the premise that it may, then we are forced to accept this conclusion: that the science-fiction novel only presents a "counterfeit . . . of present reality," to use H. Bruce Franklin's words, and, since it is a "counterfeit," then, it cannot be real (p. 3). Reality, therefore, becomes the central problem of all science fiction, since how we define and understand reality will be, in the final analysis, the determining factor in how we understand the novel. And, as we have shown, the scientist's view of reality in the eighteenth and nineteenth centuries is radically different than that presently held by contemporary mathematical physics. Indeed, as was suggested in chapter 2, reality in modern physics ceases to be a meaningful concept, and has disappeared from the "abstract lexicon of quantum physics." Yet in order to have a literature, and, especially, a literature of science fiction, we must accept the *fiction* that reality, in the sense of the world of perceptual phenomena, the world of familiar and everyday experience, is presentable and, therefore, representational in literary art. The problem becomes of particular importance in the science-fiction novel because science fiction *is* a literature which takes into *account* science and, therefore, its view of reality. And, it is in this *accounting* that the problems of plausibility and credibility arise and make science fiction, as a sub-genre of the novel, distinct and different from other forms of fiction. Gordon R. Dickson in "Plausibility in Science Fiction" suggests that "there is no question that plausibility—that . . . art of making a story worthy of belief—in science fiction makes a different and extra demand upon its author in comparison, for example, to that which an equivalent piece of historical or contemporary fiction makes upon its creator."[7]

> In all forms of story-making, imagination is required for the creation of characters, the rendering of scenes, and in the organization of the action. These three vital elements not only need to be entertaining and original, but must also convey an impression of reality, or the reader will lose faith in the story and abandon it. However, science fiction undertakes a requirement beyond these three. It contracts with its readers to provide not only these three necessary elements but also to offer an experience outside of ordinary reality; and it undertakes to make this particular experience believable—however unfamiliar or bizarre—or fail as a story. (p. 295)

Dickson makes an implicit distinction in this passage between what we might call "ordinary" reality and a nonexistent reality or a reality which "by definition, cannot call on authority of what is, or has been, actually existent" to justify itself (p. 297). The point is that science fiction must reflect in its structure and form the "reality" science "presents" and not simply the reality of sensory phenomena in which man is "trapped" by his nature or it is not science fiction. Science fiction and the science-fiction novel, therefore, must be taken as a whole, as "a manufactured reality," to borrow a phrase from Dickson (p. 297). It establishes its own rules and its own logic and these rules and this logic are the principles of science. In other words, science, in science fiction, results in a change in the very concepts of what we mean by literature, if what we mean by literature is the tradition of literary art from the Greeks to the present. Science fiction, in theory—though that theory is rarely achieved—presupposes that the everyday world with its reality will be changed by science and that a new and different reality will be created in its place. Any similarity between this new and created reality and ours, therefore, will be an extension of our own, but it will not be the same as ours. There is a classic science-fiction story which, though it pushes the direction of our argument here to an extreme, illustrates this idea of a "manufactured reality." It is *Flatland,* published in the 1880's by A. Square (a pseudonym for Edwin A. Abbott, 1838–1926), a work rarely read outside the sciences. *Flatland: A Romance of Many Dimensions* is, according to Banesh Hoffman in his "Introduction" to the sixth edition, "a stirring adventure in pure mathematics, a fantasy of strange places peopled by geometrical figures; geometrical figures that think and speak and have all too human emotions" (p. n. p.).[8] Though *Flatland* was "not conceived in the era of relativity," as Hoffman informs us, and though "it was written . . . when Einstein was a mere child and the idea of space-time lay almost a quarter of a century in the future," it does illustrate my point. It is a novel and it is a mathematical fiction and since mathematics is a science, it qualifies as science fiction. The form of the novel with respect to its narrative technique is first person presented as a memory or series of memories which the narrator recalls according to the laws and axioms of his world. This world is the world of Euclidean geometry—of two dimensions, width and breadth; consequently its title *Flatland*. In "Part 1: This World" our narrator tells us that his "world Flatland" is called that "not because we call it so, but to make its nature clearer to you, my happy readers, who are privileged to live in Space." He continues by asking us to:

> Imagine a vast sheet of paper on which straight Lines, Triangles, Squares, Pentagons, Hexagons and other figures, instead of remaining fixed in their places, move freely about, on or in the surface, but without the power of rising above or sinking below it, very much like shadows—only hard and with luminous edges—and you will then have a pretty correct notion of my country and my countrymen. Alas, a few years ago, I should have said, "my universe": but now my mind has been opened to higher views of things. (p. 4)

The point is, of course, that what constitutes reality for the Flatlanders is not ours and can never be ours. The reality of the Flatlanders is the reality of mathematical abstraction and the novel demands that we accept that mathematics is a language for describing that reality. The principles of Euclidean geometry on which *Flatland* is based have, of course, been replaced by Einstein's relativity, quantum mechanics and the Principle of Uncertainty, etc. And the principles of mathematical physics have found their way into our literature in the form of chance, indeterminacy, and probability, among others. Consequently, if science fiction must account for its science, then, its form as well as its structure must reflect the significance of the principles of science. What we mean, therefore, by the "whole" can no longer be understood in the sense in which Aristotle defined it; that is, the "whole" can no longer be understood in the sense of being *complete* like a man or a box, to use Aristotle's terms. The problem becomes a paradoxical assertion that a whole must be, according to the limitative theorems, indeterminacy, relativity, etc., incomplete—obviously a contradiction in terms or, at least it would appear on the surface to be so. The point is, of course, to paraphrase a sentence by Bertrand Russell, that "the novel and literature and literary criticism are not things, like rocks or houses; they are ways in which things behave" (Barnett, p. 15). In attempting to describe the way in which the science-fiction novel behaves I have been forced into abstractions which force us away from the fundamental structure of the novel, away from the senses, and into a series of theoretical concepts which only remove us from the creative aspects of the novel and of the inescapable and, perhaps, unexplainable nature of creation itself. And, if this problem is to be solved, then, as Susan Sontag suggests, "What is needed is a vocabulary—a descriptive, rather than prescriptive, vocabulary—for forms" (p. 159). Further, in a note to her essay Sontag tells us that "what we don't have yet is a poetics of the novel, any clear notion of the forms of narration" (p. 183). I believe Sontag is correct, for without a descriptive vocabulary for the forms of the novel I have had to take an extremely round-about method of presenting and dealing with the nature of the contemporary science-fiction novel. This method has forced me to examine at length concepts and ideas in mathematical physics which are understood with relative ease in the language of physics but when "translated" into the existing critical vocabulary and tradition of English, become difficult. However, wholism, as I conceive of it, is a way of taking into account the principles of modern mathematical physics as they exist in the science-fiction novel and for describing the indeterminate nature of all products of the imagination.

Returning to Aristotle we must now understand that the "whole" must be understood as being incomplete and broken at certain points in the novel. And as our world view encompasses such ideas as indeterminacy, relativity, and probability theory, we find ourselves in a situation analagous to that of Newton, as he "felt like a child playing at the seashore, happy whenever he found a smoother pebble or a more beautiful sea shell than usual, while the great ocean of truth lay unexplored before him" (Heisenberg, p. 123). Or, as John Weightman expressed it in Koestler's essay, "Order from Disorder," "I understand that I don't really understand what I have the illusion of understanding, since all language is no more than a mirage of comprehensibility above a sea of unknowing" (p. 64). And I am tempted to end with Samuel Delany's dictum, "Endings to be useful must be inconclusive" (p. 137).

Notes

Introduction

1. Thomas D. Clareson, "Introduction: The Critical Reception of Science Fiction." In *SF: The Other Side of Realism* (Bowling Green: Bowling Green University Popular Press, 1971), p. ix.
2. Ibid.

Chapter 1

1. Marjorie Hope Nicholson, *The Breaking of the Circle* (New York: Columbia University Press, 1962).
2. Arnold Hauser, "The Conceptions of Time in Modern Art and Science," *Partisan Review* 23 (1965), p. 320.
3. Lois and Stephen Rose, *The Shattered Ring* (Richmond, Virginia: John Knox Press, 1970).
4. Alfred North Whitehead, *Science and the Modern World* (New York: The New American Library, Inc., 1925).
5. Wayne C. Booth, *The Rhetoric of Fiction* (Chicago: University of Chicago Press, 1961).
6. Jean Paul Sartre, "François Mauriac and Freedom." In *Literary and Philosophical Essays,* trans. Annette Michelson (London, 1955), p. 16.
7. Werner Heisenberg, "The Representation of Nature in Contemporary Physics." In *The Discontinuous Universe,* eds. Sallie Sears and Georgianna W. Lord (New York: Basic Books, Inc., 1972), p. 122.
8. J. Bronowski, *The Common Sense of Science* (New York: Random House, Inc., n.d.), p. 9.
9. Gary K. Wolfe, "The Limits of Science Fiction," *Extrapolation* 14, no. 1 (December 1972), 30.
10. Judith Merril, "What Do You Mean: Science? Fiction?" In *SF: The Other Side of Realism,* ed. Thomas D. Clareson (Bowling Green, Ohio: Bowling Green University Popular Press, 1971), p. 86.

Notes for Chapter 2

11. H. Bruce Franklin, *Future Perfect: American Science Fiction of the Nineteenth Century* (New York: Oxford University Press, 1966), p. 3.

12. Brian W. Aldiss, *Billion Year Spree* (Garden City, New York: Doubleday & Company, Inc., 1973).

13. Alain Robbe-Grillet, *For A New Novel,* trans. Richard Howard, 2nd ed. (1963; rpt. New York: Grove Press, Inc., 1965), p. 32.

14. Ronald W. Clark, *Einstein: The Life and Times* (New York: The World Publishing Company, 1971), p. 75.

15. David Daiches, *The Novel and the Modern World* (Chicago: University of Chicago Press, 1960), p. 7.

16. Jerome Hamilton Buckley, *The Triumph of Time: A Study of the Victorian Concepts of Time, History, Progress, and Decadence* (Cambridge, Mass.: Belknap Press, 1966), p. 7.

17. Stanley Edger Hyman, *The Armed Vision* (New York: Random House, Inc., 1955), p. 3.

Chapter 2

1. Samuel R. Delany, *The Einstein Intersection* (New York: Ace Books, 1967).

2. Reginald Bretnor, "Science Fiction in the Age of Space." In *Science Fiction, Today and Tomorrow,* ed. Reginald Bretnor (New York: Harper & Row, 1974), p. 151.

3. Robbe-Grillet, *For a New Novel,* p. 17.

4. Charles W. Misner, Kip S. Thorne, and John A. Wheeler, *Gravitation* (San Francisco: W. H. Freeman and Company, 1973), p. 71.

5. Charles Olson, "Projective Verse." In *Human Universe and Other Essays,* ed. Donald Allen (New York: Grove Press, Inc., 1967), p. 52.

6. Martin Dyck, "Relativity in Physics and in Fiction." In *Studies in German Literature of the Nineteenth and Twentieth Centuries,* ed. Siegfried Mews (Chapel Hill: University of North Carolina Press, 1970), p. 174.

7. Thomas D. Clareson, "The Other Side of Realism." In *SF: The Other Side of Realism,* ed. Thomas D. Clareson (Bowling Green: Bowling Green University Popular Press, 1971), p. 22.

8. Ibid.

9. Thomas S. Kuhn, *The Structure of Scientific Revolutions* (Chicago: University of Chicago Press, 1970), p. 4.

10. Lincoln Barnett, *The Universe and Dr. Einstein* (New York: Bantam Books, Inc., 1973), p. 113.

11. Bronowski, *The Common Sense of Science,* p. 69.

12. Robbe-Grillet, p. 74.

13. Witold Gombrowicz, quoted in "Introduction," by Jacques Ehrmann, *Structuralism,* ed. Jacques Ehrmann (New York: Doubleday & Company, Inc., 1970), p. vii.

14. Howard DeLong, "Unsolved Problems in Arithmetic," *Scientific American* 224, no. 3 (March 1971), 58-59.

15. Wallace Stevens, "Imagination as Value." In *The Necessary Angel* (New York: Vintage-Knopf, 1951), p. 140.

16. Merril, p. 56.

17. Stephen Scobie, "Different Mazes: Mythology in Samuel R. Delany's 'The Einstein Intersection,' " *Riverside Quarterly* 5, no. 1 (1973), p. 12.

18. Geoffrey Hartman, Structuralism: The Anglo-American Adventure." In *Structuralism*, ed. Jacques Ehrmann (New York: Doubleday & Company, Inc., 1970), p. 152.

19. Ibid., p. 143.

20. Ibid.

21. Sallie Sears and Georgianna W. Lord, "Introduction." In *The Discontinuous Universe*, eds. Sallie Sears and Georgianna W. Lord (New York: Basic Books, Inc., 1972), p. v.

22. Booth, pp. 151-52.

23. Ibid., pp. 153-54.

24. Mark Schorer, *The World We Imagine* (New York: Farrar, Straus and Giroux, 1968), p. 10.

Chapter 3

1. Gregory T. Polletta, "The Place and Performance of Criticism." In *Issues in Contemporary Literary Criticism,* ed. Gregory T. Polletta (Boston: Little, Brown, and Company, 1973), p. 21.

2. Ibid.

3. George Brecht, "Change-Imagery." In *The Discontinuous Universe,* eds. Sallie Sears and Georgianna W. Lord (New York: Basic Books, Inc., 1972), p. 84.

4. Robbe-Grillet, *For A New Novel.*

5. "Static Scrutiny," *The London Times Literary Supplement* (October 3, 1968), p. 1137.

6. Walter Tevis, *The Man Who Fell To Earth* (New York: Lancer Books, 1963).

7. J. Bronowski, *The Common Sense of Science* (New York: Random House, Inc., 1973), p. 60.

8. J. Bronowski, "The Discovery of Form." In *Science and Literature,* ed. Edward M. Jennings (Garden City, New York: Doubleday & Company, Inc., 1970), p. 9.

9. A. M. Arthurs, *Probability Theory* (New York: Dover Publications, Inc., 1965), p. 9.

10. Brian W. Aldiss, *Report on Probability A* (New York: Lancer Books, 1968).

11. "Static Scrutiny," p. 1137.

12. Ibid.

13. Maurice Merleau-Ponty, "What is Phenomenology?" In *Phenomenology: The Philos-*

Notes for Chapter 5

      ophy of Edmund Husserl and Its Interpretation (Garden City, New York: Doubleday & Company, Inc., 1967), p. 361.

14. Thomas S. Kuhn, *The Structure of Scientific Revolutions* (Chicago: The University of Chicago Press, 1970), p. 114.

15. Werner Heisenberg, "The Representation of Nature in Contemporary Physics." In *The Discontinuous Universe,* eds. Sallie Sears and Georgianna W. Lord (New York: Basic Books, Inc., 1972), pp. 128–29.

16. Michael Crichton, *The Andromeda Strain* (New York: Dell Publishing Co., Inc., 1970), p. 230.

17. Maurice Natanson, *Literature, Philosophy, And The Social Sciences* (The Hague: Martinus Nijhoff, 1962), p. 9.

Chapter 4

1. Aldiss, *Billion Year Spree,* p. 145.
2. Wolfe, "The Limits of Science Fiction," p. 34.
3. Bronowski, *The Common Sense of Science,* pp. 120–30.
4. Fred Hoyle, *The Black Cloud* (New York: New American Library, Inc., 1959).
5. M. A. Goldberg, "Chronology, Character and the Human Condition: A Reappraisal of the Modern Novel." In *Critical Approaches to Fiction,* eds., Shiv. K. Kumar and Keith McKean (New York: McGraw-Hill Book Company, 1968). p. 14.
6. Martin Gardner, "Can Time Go Backward?" *Scientific American* 216, no. 1 (January 1967), p. 98.
7. Barnett, p. 46.
8. A. A. Mendilow, *Time and the Novel* (New York: Humanities Press, 1965), p. 14.
9. Robbe-Grillet, p. 155.
10. Kurt Vonnegut, Jr., *Slaughterhouse-Five or The Children's Crusade* (1969; rpt. New York: Dell Publishing Co., Inc., 1971), p. 1.
11. Tony Tanner, "The Uncertain Messenger: A Study of the Novels of Kurt Vonnegut, Jr." *Critical Quarterly* 11, no. 4 (Winter 1969), p. 310.
12. Booth, p. 73.
13. Delany, p. 137.
14. Daiches, p. 7.
15. Merril, p. 72.

Chapter 5

1. Arthur Koestler, "Order from Disorder," *Harper's* 249, no. 1490 (July 1974), p. 64.
2. Rene Wellek, *Concepts of Criticism* (New Haven and London: Yale University Press, 1963), p. 65.

3. William K. Wimsatt, Jr. and Cleanth Brooks, *Literary Criticism: A Short History* (New York: Alfred A. Knopf, 1967), p. 29.

4. John Dewey, *Intelligence in the Modern World: John Dewey's Philosophy,* ed. Joseph Ratner (New York: Random House, Inc., 1939), p. 640.

5. Clareson, "The Other Side of Realism," pp. 1, 5.

6. Stanley Edgar Hyman, "Afterword." In *A Clockwork Orange,* by Anthony Burgess (New York: W. W. Norton & Company, Inc., 1963), p. 179.

7. Gordon R. Dickson, "Plausibility in Science Fiction." In *Science Fiction: Today and Tomorrow,* ed. Reginald Bretnor (New York: Harper & Row, 1974), p. 295.

8. Edwin A. Abbott, *Flatland: A Romance of Many Dimensions,* 6th ed. (1884; rpt. New York: Dover Publications, Inc., 1952).

Bibliography

Abbott, Edwin A. *Flatland: A Romance of Many Dimensions*. 6th ed. New York: Dover Publications, Inc., 1952.
Aldiss, Brian W. *Billion Year Spree: The True History of Science Fiction*. Garden City, New York: Doubleday & Co., Inc., 1973.
―――. *Report on Probability A*. New York: Lancer Books, Inc., 1968.
Armytage, W. H. G. *Yesterday's Tomorrows: A Historical Survey of Future Societies*. London: Routledge & Kegan Paul, 1968.
Arthurs, A. M. *Probability Theory*. New York: Dover Publications, Inc., 1965.
Auerback, Eric. *Mimesis: The Representation of Reality in Western Literature*. Princeton, New Jersey: Princeton University Press, 1953.
Barnett, Lincoln. *The Universe and Dr. Einstein*. New York: Bantam Books, Inc., 1973.
Beardsley, Monroe C. *Aesthetics From Classical Greece to the Present: A Short History*. New York: The Macmillan Company, 1966.
―――. *Aesthetics: Problems in the Philosophy of Criticism*. New York: Harcourt, Brace and Co., 1958.
Booth, Wayne C. *The Rhetoric of Fiction*. Chicago: University of Chicago Press, 1961.
Brecht, George. "Chance Imagery." *The Discontinuous Universe*. Eds. Sallie Sears and Georgianna W. Lord. New York: Basic Books, Inc., 1972, pp. 76-96.
Bretnor, Reginald. "Science Fiction in the Age of Space." *Science Fiction: Today and Tomorrow*. Ed. Reginald Bretnor. New York: Harper & Row, 1974, p. 151.
Bronowski, J. *The Common Sense of Science*. New York: Random House, Inc., n.d.
―――. "The Discovery of Form." *Science and Literature: New Lenses for Criticism*. Ed. Edward M. Jennings. Garden City, New York: Anchor Books, 1970, pp. 1-11.
Buckley, Jerome Hamilton. *The Triumph of Time: A Study of Time, History, Progress, and Decadence*. Cambridge, Mass. Belknap Press, 1966.
Burgess, Anthony. *A Clockwork Orange*. New York: W. W. Norton & Co., Inc., 1963.
Clareson, Thomas D. *Extrapolation: A Science-Fiction Newsletter*. 10 vols. New York: Johnson Reprint Corp., 1970.
―――. *Science Fiction Criticism: An Annotated Checklist*. Kent, Ohio: Kent State University Press, 1972.
―――, ed. "The Other Side of Realism." *SF: The Other Side of Realism*. Bowling Green: Bowling Green University Popular Press, 1971, pp. 2-28.
Clark, Ronald W. *Einstein: The Life and Times*. New York: The World Publishing Co., 1971.
Crichton, Michael. *The Andromeda Strain*. New York: Dell Publishing Co., Inc., 1971.
Daiches, David. *The Novel and the Modern World*. Chicago: University of Chicago Press, 1960.
Delany, Samuel R. *The Einstein Intersection*. New York: Ace Books, 1967.

DeLong, Howard. "Unsolved Problems in Arithmetic." *Scientific American* 224 (March 1971), pp. 50–60.
Dewey, John. *Art as Experience.* New York: Capricorn Books, 1958.
―――――. *Intelligence in the Modern World: John Dewey's Philosophy.* Ed. Joseph Ratner. New York: Random House, Inc., 1939.
Dickson, Gordon R. "Plausibility in Science Fiction." *Science Fiction: Today and Tomorrow.* Ed. Reginald Bretnor. New York: Harper & Row, 1974, pp. 295–306.
Dyck, Martin. "Relativity in Physics and Fiction." *Studies In German Literature of the Nineteenth and Twentieth Centuries.* Ed. Siegfried Mews. Chapel Hill: University of North Carolina Press, 1970, pp. 174–85.
Ehrmann, Jacques, ed. *Structuralism.* New York: Doubleday & Co., Inc., 1970, pp. vii–xi.
Extrapolation: A Journal of Science Fiction and Fantasy. The Journal of the MLA Seminar on Science Fiction. Ed. Thomas D. Clareson. Wooster, Ohio: College of Wooster.
Franklin, H. Bruce. *Future Perfect: American Science Fiction of the Nineteenth Century.* New York: Oxford University Press, 1966.
Fraser, J. T., Haber, F.C. and Muller, G. H. *The Study of Time.* New York: Springer-Verlag, 1972.
Gardner, Martin. "Can Time Go Backward?" *Scientific American* 216 (January 1967), pp. 98–108.
Goldberg, M. A. "Chronology, Character and the Human Condition: A Reappraisal of the Modern Novel." *Critical Approaches to Fiction.* Ed. Shiv. K. Kumar and Keith McKean. New York: McGraw-Hill Book Co., 1968, pp. 13–15.
Hartman, Geoffrey. "Structuralism: The Anglo-American Adventure." *Structuralism.* Ed. Jacques Ehrmann. New York: Doubleday & Co., Inc., 1970, pp. 137–58.
Hauser, Arnold. "The Conceptions of Time in Modern Art and Science." *Partisan Review* 23 (1965), 320–33.
Heisenberg, Werner. "The Representation of Nature in Contemporary Physics." *The Discontinuous Universe.* Eds. Sallie Sears and Georgianna W. Lord. New York: Basic Books, Inc., 1972, pp. 122–35.
Hemingway, Ernest. *Green Hills of Africa.* New York: Charles Scribner's Sons, 1935.
Hildick, Wallace. "Tiny Facts." *The Listener* 79 (1968), p. 579.
Hoyle, Fred. *The Black Cloud.* New York: The New American Library of World Literature, Inc., 1959.
Hyman, Stanley Edgar. *The Armed Vision: A Study in the Methods of Modern Literary Criticism.* New York: Random House, Inc., 1955.
―――――. "Afterword." *A Clockwork Orange.* New York: W. W. Norton & Co., Inc., 1963, pp. 177–82.
Kazin, Alfred. "The War Novel From Mailer to Vonnegut." *Saturday Review* 54 (1971), pp. 13–15, 36.
Klinowitz, Jerome and Somer, John. *The Vonnegut Statement.* New York: Dell Publishing Co., Inc., 1973.
Koestler, Arthur. "Order from Disorder." *Harper's* 249 (1974), pp. 54–64.
Kohl, Herbert. *The Age of Complexity.* New York: The New American Library of World Literature, Inc., 1965.
Kuhn, Thomas S. *The Structure of Scientific Revolutions.* Chicago: University of Chicago Press, 1970.
Langer, Susanne K. *Philosophy in a New Key.* New York: The New American Library of World Literature, Inc., 1958.
Mendilow, A. A. *Time and the Novel.* New York: Humanities Press, 1965.

Merleau-Ponty, Maurice. "What is Phenomenology?" *Phenomenology: The Philosophy of Edmund Husserl and Its Interpretation.* Garden City, New York: Anchor Books, 1967.
Merril, Judith. "What Do You Mean: Science? Fiction?" *SF: The Other Side of Realism.* Ed. Thomas D. Clareson. Bowling Green: Bowling Green University Popular Press, 1971, pp. 53-95.
Misner, Charles W., Thorne, Kip S., and Wheeler, John A. *Gravitation.* San Francisco: W. H. Freeman and Co., 1973.
Moskowitz, Sam. *Explorers of the Infinite: Shapers of Science Fiction.* Westport, Conn.: Hyperion Press, Inc., 1974.
_____. *Seekers of Tomorrow: Masters of Modern Science Fiction.* Westport, Conn.: Hyperion Press, Inc., 1974.
Nagel, Ernest and Newman, James R. *Goedel's Proof.* New York: New York University Press, 1960.
Natanson, Maurice. *Literature, Philosophy, and the Social Sciences.* The Hague: Martinus Nijhoff, 1962.
Nicholson, Marjorie Hope. *The Breaking of the Circle.* New York: Columbia University Press, 1962.
_____. *Voyages to the Moon.* New York: The Macmillan Company, 1960.
O'Connor, Gerald W. "The Function of Time Travel in Vonnegut's Slaughterhouse-Five." *Riverside Quarterly* 5 (August 1972), pp. 206-7.
Olderman, Raymond M. "Beyond the Waste Land: A Study of the American Novel in the Nineteen-Sixties." Ph.D. dissertation, Indiana University, 1969.
Olson, Charles. *Human Universe and Other Essays.* Ed. Donald Allen. New York: Grove Press, Inc., 1967.
Polletta, Gregory T. *Issues in Contemporary Literary Criticism.* Boston: Little, Brown and Co., 1973.
Riverside Quarterly. Ed. Leland Sapiro. Regina, Sask., Canada.
Robbe-Grillet, Alain. *For a New Novel: Essays on Fiction.* Trans. Richard Howard. New York: Grove Press, Inc., 1965.
Rose, Lois and Rose, Stephen. *The Shattered Ring: Science Fiction and the Quest for Meaning.* Richmond, Va.: John Knox Press, 1970.
Sartre, Jean Paul. "François Mauriac and Freedom." *Literary and Philosophical Essays.* Trans. Annette Michelson. London (1965), pp. 1-16.
Schatt, Stanley. "The World Picture of Kurt Vonnegut, Jr." Ph.D. dissertation, University of Southern California, 1970.
Schorer, Mark. *The World We Imagine.* New York: Farrar, Straus and Giroux, 1968.
Science-Fiction Studies. Ed. R. D. Mullen and Darko Suvin. Terre Haute, Ind.: Indiana State University.
Scobie, Stephen. "Different Mazes: Mythology in Samuel R. Delany's *The Einstein Intersection.*" *Riverside Quarterly* 5 (1973), 12-18.
Sears, Sallie and Lord, Georgianna W. "Introduction." *The Discontinuous Universe.* Eds. Sallie Sears and Georgianna W. Lord. New York: Basic Books, Inc., 1972, pp. iv-vii.
Somer, John L. "Quick-Stasis: The Rite of Initiation in the Novels of Kurt Vonnegut, Jr." Ph.D. dissertation, Northern Illinois University, 1971.
Stevens, Wallace. "Imagination as Value." *The Necessary Angle.* New York: Vintage-Knopf, 1951, pp. 133-56.
Tanner, Tony. "The Uncertain Messenger: A Study of the Novels of Kurt Vonnegut, Jr." *Critical Quarterly* 11 (Winter 1969), 297-315.
Tevis, Walter. *The Man Who Fell To Earth.* New York: Lancer Books, Inc., 1963.

Vonnegut, Kurt, Jr. *Slaughterhouse-Five or The Children's Crusade: A Duty Dance With Death.* New York: Dell Publishing Co., Inc., 1971.
Watt, Ian. *The Rise of the Novel: Studies in Defoe, Richardson and Fielding.* Berkeley and Los Angeles: University of California Press, 1965.
Wellek, Rene. *Concepts of Criticism.* New Haven and London: Yale University Press, 1963.
────────. *A History of Modern Criticism: 1750-1950.* New Haven: Yale University Press, 1965.
────────. *Theory of Literature.* New York: Harcourt, Brace & World, Inc., 1956.
White, Morton. *The Age of Analysis.* New York: The New American Library of World Literature, Inc., 1963.
Whitehead, Alfred North. *Science and the Modern World.* New York: The New American Library of World Literature, Inc., 1925.
Wimsatt, William K. and, Brooks, Cleanth. *Literary Criticism: A Short History.* New York: Alfred A. Knopf, 1967.
Wolfe, Gary K. "The Limits of Science Fiction." *Extrapolation* 14 (December 1972), 30-37.
Young, B. A. "Space Time." *Punch* 254 (1968), 865.
Zeman, Jiri, ed. *Time in Science and Philosophy: An International Study of Some Current Problems.* New York: Elsevier, 1972.

Index

Abbott, Edwin A. (A. Square)
  Flatland, 101-2
Aldiss, Brian W., xiv,7,48,73,89
  See also *Report on Probability A*
Aristotle, 94,102,103
  Physics, 93
Armytage, W. H. G., xiv
Arthurs, A. M.
  on models, 52-53,54
Asimov, Isaac, 5,6,73

Barnett, Lincoln, 9,103
  on Einsteinian concept of reality, 22-23,24
  on Einsteinian concept of time, 73,75-76, 78-79
Booth, Wayne C., 16,20
  on first person narrators, 39,77
  on narrative technique, 2,3,4
Brecht, George, 46-47
Bretnor, Reginald, xiv,5
Bronowski, Jacob, 17,97
  on modern science, 4,7,24,52
  on Newtonian physics, 8,9-10
Brooks, Cleanth, 93
Buckley, Jerome, 11
Burgess, Anthony
  A Clockwork Orange, 99-100

Clareson, Thomas D., xii,xiv,98-99
Clark, Ronald W., 8,19
Coleridge, S. T., 11,92
Conant, James B., 21,98
Copernicus, Nikolaus, 1
Crichton, Michael
  The Andromeda Strain, 62

Daiches, David, 89
Defoe, Daniel
  Moll Flanders, 10
Delany, Samuel F., 89,103
  See also *The Einstein Intersection*

Delong, Howard, 29,30,37
Descartes, René, 13,15
Dewey, John, 95-96
Dickens, Charles
  David Copperfield, 74-75
Dickson, Gordon R., 101
Dyck, Martin, 21,22,25,26

Einstein, Albert, 3,13,23,102
  and *The Einstein Intersection*, 32-33, 36,37
  on mathematics and fiction, 19
  on space-time continuum, 78-79
  See also Relativity theory
Einstein Intersection, The, 16,19,48,52,87,95
  difference in, 31-32,39,41
  Einsteinian and Goedelian physics in, 29, 32-33,34,37,38,39,42,45
  first person narration in, 39-42
  form of, 20-21,27,42,47-48
  mathematical physics and fiction in, 26-27
  myth in, 27-28,31,35-39
  narrator's perceptions in, 23,25,32,39,41
  view of creative process in, 21,29,33-34, 37,39,40
Extrapolation, xiv

Form in the novel, 47
  definition of, 20,46
  organic, 42,46,47,91-93,94
  wholistic, 47-48,76,93-95,102-3
Franklin, H. Bruce, 6, 100

Galilei, Galileo, 1,12
Gardner, Martin, 75
Gernsback, Hugo, 5
  Ralph 124C 41+, 7
Goedel, Kurt
  limitative theorems of, 29-30,33,36,37, 43,45,102

116   Index

Goethe, Johann Wolfgang von, 55,56
Goldberg, M. A., 74-75
Gombrowicz, Witold, 27

Hartman, Geoffrey, 38,91-92,93
Hassan, Ihab, 46
Hauser, Arnold, 1,8
Heinlein, Robert, 5
Heisenberg, Werner, 45,58,72,103
   on changes in modern science, 13-15
   on modern art, 1,4,5,12
   Uncertainty Principle of, 16,24,48,71,102
Hemingway, Ernest
   The Green Hills of Africa, 77
Hoffman, Banesh, 101-2
Howells, William Dean, 98-99
Hoyle, Fred
   The Black Cloud, 74
Hyman, Edgar Stanley, 100
   on literary criticism, 12,96-97

James, William, 22
Joyce, James
   Finnegan's Wake, 75

Kepler, Johannes, 1,12
Koestler, Arthur, 91,92,93,94,103
Kuhn, Thomas, 22,23,56

Limitative theorems. *See* Goedel, Kurt
Lord, Georgianna W., 45

Mathematical physics, modern, xiv-xv,91
   and fiction, 21-27,93,102,103
   and narrative technique in science fiction, 1-7,16
   See also Science, modern
Mauriac, François, 2,3,5,7,11
Mechanistic world view, 8-10,12-15,93, 94,99
Mendilow, A. A., 76
Merleau-Ponty, Maurice, 55
Merril, Judith, 6,34,89
Moskowitz, Sam, xiv

Narrative technique
   first person, 3,7,10
   influence of modern science on, 1,3-17
   omniscient, 3,7,9,72
Natanson, Maurice, 69
Newton, Sir Isaac, 1,4,12,13,95,103
   Philosophiae Naturalis Principia Mathematica, 8
   See also Mechanistic world view
Nicholson, Marjorie Hope, 1

Olson, Charles, 20,46

Probability theory, 16,43,45,46-47,102,103
   in *Report on Probability A*, 48-49,52-54, 71,72,94

Quantum theory. *See* Relativity theory

Reality
   and modern mathematical physics, 21-22, 25,26,100
   as represented in science fiction, 16-17, 98,100-1
   nineteenth-century view of, 98-99
Relativity theory, 23,43,80,94,102,103
   and fiction, 3,24,95
   and observation, 7,13,15,26,32,52,64
   and *The Einstein Intersection*, 16, 32-33,45
   and time, 73,75-76,79
Report on Probability A, 16,43,45,76, 94,95
   form of, 48,71,72
   Holman Hunt's "The Hireling Shepherd" in, 49-50,63-64,65-68,70,72
   metaphor in, 51-52
   point of view in, 60,64,72
   probability theory in, 48-49,51,52-54, 71,72
   process of observation in, 55-65,68, 70-71,72
Richardson, Samuel, 10
Riverside Quarterly, xiv
Robbe-Grillet, Alain, 48,53
   on earlier fiction, 7-8,9,11
   on metaphor, 51,52
   on the modern novel, 17,19,25,49, 81,88
   on time, 76,78
Romantic poets, 93
Rose, Lois and Stephen, 1
Russell, Bertrand, 102-3

Sartre, Jean-Paul, 6,7,11,12,25
   on narrative technique, 2-4
Schorer, Mark, 42
Science, definition of, 95-96
Science, modern
   as myth in *The Einstein Intersection*, 36-37,39
   and reality, 21-22,25,26,100
   changes in, 4-5,6,12-16,93
   effect on literary art of, 1,93,95,97
   See also Mathematical physics, modern
Science fiction
   criticism of, xiii-xiv,7

lack of experiment in, 5-7,9,74
narrative technique in, 1-17
this study of, xiii,xiv,xv
time sequence in, 6,7,73,75
view of reality in, 16-17,98,100
wholistic theory of, 93-95,97-98,102-3
Science-Fiction Studies, xiv
Scobie, Stephen, 41
  on myth in *The Einstein Intersection,* 27, 33-36,37,38-39
Sears, Sallie, 45
Slaughterhouse-Five, 7,16 95
  concept of time in, 73,75,76,79,80-81, 88-89
  fictive "I" (narrator) in, 76-78,79-80
  function of "Chapter One" in, 81-88
  references to history in, 85-86
  structure of, 76,80,81,88-89
Sontag, Susan, 99,103
Space
  Newtonian conception of, 8-9
Space-time, Einstein's concept of, 16, 78-79,102
Stevens, Wallace, 34

Tanner, Tony, 76-77

Tevis, Walter
  The Man Who Fell to Earth, 52
Time
  Einsteinian concept of, 73,75-76,78
  in the eighteenth- and nineteenth-century novel, 10-11,74-75
  in *Slaughterhouse-Five,* 73,75,76,79, 80-81,88-89
  Newtonian concept of, 8-9,75,78

Uncertainty, Principle of, 16,24,48,71,102

Verne, Jules, 5,74
Vonnegut, Kurt, Jr., 76-77
  See also Slaughterhouse-Five

Weightman, John, 103
Wellek, Rene, 92-93
Wells, H. G., 5,74
  The Time Machine, 73
Whitehead, Alfred North, 1,23
Wholistic theory of art, 93-95,97-98, 102-3
Wimsatt, William K., Jr., 93,94
Wolfe, Gary K. 5,7,73,74

LIBRARY
as soon as you
to avoid